TALES FROM A FINANCIAL HOT MESS

Frances Cook is a reformed money mess, currently managing podcasts for the *New Zealand Herald*, Newstalk ZB, and RadioSport. She is best known for hosting the personal finance podcast 'Cooking the Books', one of New Zealand's most popular podcasts.

Gaining a Master's in Media Studies from Victoria University of Wellington, Frances went on to work as a journalist, first at Radio Live then Newstalk ZB, before moving to cover politics for ZB. She more recently made the switch to work at the *Herald*, first as a senior multimedia journalist, and now in her podcast role.

As well as hosting 'Cooking the Books', Frances also hosts 'The Front Page', which goes behind the scenes of the biggest investigations out of the *Herald* newsroom. She is the executive producer of podcasts 'Speaking Secrets' and 'Trip Notes', with others in the pipeline. She is a regular commentator for Newstalk ZB radio shows, particularly on politics and personal finance matters.

FRANCES COOK

TALES FROM A FINANCIAL HOT MESS

The realest guide to money... and how to have more of it

RANDOM HOUSE NEW ZEALAND

Contents

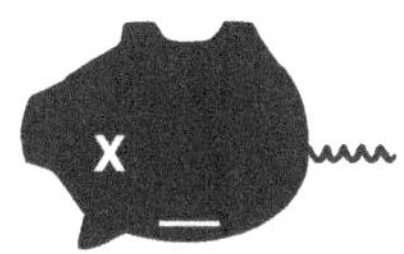

The best time to plant a tree was twenty years ago.
The second-best time is today.
Unknown

Do what you can,
with what you've got,
where you are.
Squire Bill Widener

Introduction

FOR YEARS I HAD a problem. I wasn't good with money. And it was affecting everything around me.

This isn't one of those 'I was $100,000 in debt, got out of it in one year, and you can too' stories. I was just . . . mediocre. Chugging along. Praying for a pay rise, getting one, then somehow not getting ahead. Impulse-buying things I knew I shouldn't, feeling bad, then hiding it from my husband. Not allowing myself a credit card, because I feared debt, feared my own relationship with money.

I knew I should have been doing better. I just had no clue where to start, and I certainly didn't realise I could have been living a much better life on the same money.

What I did have was a plan. Or, as my husband would say, rolling his eyes, I cooked up a scheme. I like schemes.

I decided to learn more about money, but on company time. Because here's the thing about being a journalist: the pay is rubbish, but the perks are amazing – like being able to interview the country's top financial minds for a personal finance podcast, while actually asking questions on how to fix my own money situation, which is exactly what I did.

This book isn't me pretending I've now become a financial expert. I've learned a lot, but I'm no financial adviser. I'm also not pretending my situation is the same as everyone else's; that would be silly. I'm an average person, who earns a pretty average wage, who doesn't have a degree in business, but who managed to turn around my money relationship. I am now doing much, much better in life, with what I already had.

I interviewed a whole bunch of smart money people and extracted the best of their wisdom, which I'm sharing here along with how it made a difference in my life. Some of it will hopefully be helpful to you. I hope that it might give you the confidence to start your own journey to doing better with your money. Then again, some of it may just make you laugh at the dumb assumptions I used to have, and that's okay too.

MOST OF US HAVE a vague feeling that we should be doing better with what we already have, and I'm afraid that suspicion is right for all but the smallest minority of cases. The figures back that up. ANZ's 2018 Financial Futures research showed that about three quarters of New Zealanders felt they were doing okay in terms of getting by day to day, but only 30 per cent of us feel like we have a handle on investing and getting ready for retirement.

That big gap in knowledge can weigh on us. Sure, we're getting by today, but what about tomorrow? What if the unexpected happens and changes things today? Just don't think about it.

If you've ever had someone stand in front of you, telling you not to think about a pink elephant, you'll know the only thing you can then think about is a pink elephant. So despite our best efforts not to think about it, that knowledge gap does weigh on us.

New Zealand Treasury figures from 2016 show that younger people are saving more today than the generation before them did when they were young. Treasury themselves said it was probably a response to the more uncertain times we're living in. It's harder to get a full-time job now, nobody knows if there will be a pension by the time we retire, and home ownership feels more and more out of reach. As a result, the average person saves more out of a vague, disquieting sense of panic. But they don't know what to do with that money.

To which I would say: don't put it all in a savings account. Invest. Make your money go to work while you stay in bed. Break the chains from the nine-to-five job and the need for a pension. If they're there, great, but we don't have to rely on them if we put a plan in place for our money. You can and should be the one in control, and once you take control of your money, you'll be amazed how many other things in your life fall into place.

Investing can and should make the lives of ordinary people easier. When you know what you're aiming for, it's a lot easier to do that other boring stuff like budgeting and saving in order to get yourself to the investments. You know that money will come back to you once you've put it somewhere smart.

The problem is nobody tells you where to start. Nobody tells you the easy, lazy ways to do it, so that it doesn't take over your life. You don't need a degree in this personal finance stuff, even though it looks that way from the outside.

This book deliberately tackles a variety of money topics in a particular order. You can't put the roof on your house if you haven't built the walls yet, and you can't put up walls before the foundations are down. Nobody waxes lyrical about how much they love their home's foundations, but without them, you won't have that pretty kitchen for long. This book follows the order in which I addressed my own money issues, and I'm pretty sure that order will work for most other people.

That said, this is a judgement-free zone. Money is a loaded topic, where emotion can run high. It's easy to say: 'Here are the rules, live by them and all your problems will be solved.' That doesn't take into account the fact that not everything is within our control. A lot is though, and changing the parts that I could has changed my life.

When I decided to stop cringing with guilt, to stop ignoring my bank account as if that would somehow change the facts of what I'd spent, my life genuinely changed. My relationship with my husband changed. There was more trust. My relationship with my bosses changed, as I became more focused on what I wanted and why. My relationship with friends and family changed – as I became more open about money, they also felt they could talk about their own struggles. My relationship with my own future changed, as I felt more in control and able to relax.

I realised money wasn't a mysterious number in my bank account, nor was it the key to happiness – but it sure helped bring me happiness when I treated it right.

1.

Rehab won't work until you're ready to get sober

I VIVIDLY REMEMBER THE day it was pointed out to me that I was hopeless with money. As they say, the truth hurts, and this particular conversation has seared its way into my long-term memory.

Until that day, I'd done a good job of deluding myself. For a long time, I had the good excuse that I was broke. There were tough times growing up, which were followed by the long student years when I worked part-time, but still struggled with Wellington rents. Then I was into the workforce, but in the notoriously low-wage media industry and with a student loan to boot.

For several years, I reasoned that my only problem was the amount of money coming in. (This was a problem, sure, but if it was the only one, you wouldn't hear about rich celebrities landing in court for not paying their debts. More on that later.) I figured if I could just get a big enough pay rise, my problems would be solved.

To give me my one bit of credit, one area where I was doing okay was in negotiating a raise. I was happily shameless about taking each and every opportunity to ask for more money. Performance review? Pay me more, please. Change of job or responsibilities? Pay me more, please.

I'd even managed to make it up to the average New Zealand wage. Yes, seriously. Journalists really don't earn much. Even though some people manage to raise a family on that money, there I was still constantly running out of funds.

One day, I was sitting at home, whining to my husband, Ben, that I literally had no money. There was a full week to go until I was paid, but I didn't even have a dollar. I was going stir crazy, so was hoping to persuade him to take me out for a coffee.

Ben is kinder than I deserve, so we were soon on our way to a café where he would not only shout me a coffee, but also some cake that I would say we needed.

But while my husband may be kind, he's also not one to mince words.

'You remember that you get paid more than me, right?'

It was delivered ever-so-casually, as we drove to the café.

'We also pay the same amount towards our mortgage, food, bills . . .' he continued to muse aloud. 'And yet you run out of money every month. Meanwhile, I'm debt free with savings.'

I rolled my eyes, wondering if this 'free' coffee came with too high a price tag. But he wasn't even done yet. He delivered a cheeky smirk in my direction before letting loose with his final, smug, zing. 'You should try it some time. I'm quite enjoying being a good little saver.'

Ouch. The worst thing about brutal honesty is how you're left with no comebacks to hide behind. Luckily, he left the matter there and he survives to this day with all limbs still attached.

I'm a proud person, but once I stopped sulking, I started thinking. Money had been a taboo topic for a long time, even between me and my husband. While I'd always known he didn't exactly approve of my money habits, he'd never been this blunt.

Something in this gentle confrontation stirred up a dormant worry that *I* was actually the biggest problem in the equation, and that not talking about it was only making it worse. The silence meant that even if I wanted to do something about it, I wasn't sure where to start.

There was also a bigger reason that I was finally ready to listen to Ben. I'd just had quite a fright on the career front. At that point, I was still in denial about how big of a near-miss it had been, but I knew it deep down.

I had been headhunted for a job that was promising satisfying work for a reputable employer, with a giant pay increase. I was tempted. I went as far as handing in my notice at work. Then, at the last minute, my current employer made a good counter-offer, so I stuck with them.

The job I was first offered eventually went to someone I knew through a friend of a friend, which is how I came to hear about my near miss. Just like they had for me, the other employer had talked a big game and convinced her to quit her current role. Then, the new role never materialised. The friend of a friend found herself unemployed at short notice, after being poached for a job that disappeared into thin air.

The news of what had happened to her shook me. If that had been me, I could have lost everything. I had very little in the way of savings, maybe a couple of hundred dollars. I certainly had no investments. I was committed to a mortgage, one that my husband couldn't pay for on his own. I had absolutely no financial cushion if something was to go wrong at short notice. My greed when I was offered that job could have left us homeless and with ruined credit because I had no plan to survive more than a couple of weeks without steady income.

When my husband pointed out to me that I should have been doing better with what I had, I was finally ready to listen because I'd just had a demonstration of the need for an emergency plan. It turns out you're sometimes offered the world, only to have it all snatched away and you should be prepared for that.

I didn't want to be a wage slave anymore. I wanted to provide my own security, to know that if times got tough I could survive. I wanted multiple emergency levers to pull on to make sure I got through life's difficulties, that my loved ones did well, and that I wouldn't get into trouble and pull anyone else down with me.

Most people would rather talk about the details of their sex life before having an honest conversation about money, but Ben laying the problem bare meant I couldn't ignore it any longer. I was useless with money; there were no two ways about it.

My salary may have seemed modest to some, but it was also the highest it had ever been and plenty of others manage to get by with less. Hell, I'd got by with less in the past. Yet there I was, still stuck in the same place. I still couldn't make my pay last the month. I still wasn't making any plans for the future.

I had a spending problem, I knew that much. I wanted good clothes, and I wanted to go out for food and drinks, and I wanted a nice house. I didn't just have one vice. I had almost all of them.

I also knew that I needed help. Money was something that I never truly felt comfortable with. It was a bunch of mythical numbers that came and went from my account each month, and that I wasn't quite sure what to do with. I blew it on quick hits of instant gratification, which were followed by longer hits of guilt for spending on silly things. Part of me suspected the problem was that I didn't know where to start.

If any of this sounds at all familiar to you, it's because we're not alone. The Commission for Financial Capability surveyed 4000 people for its 2018 Financial Capability Barometer. They found that 27 per cent of people with a household income over $100,000 had high-interest debt to third-tier lenders, like payday lenders. Surely, you would think those people were earning enough that nearly a third of them wouldn't be in hot water with loan sharks. And yet, there they were. It turns out there are plenty of people on six-figure salaries who complain they're broke, or people who earn a bit less who should still be comfortable, yet aren't. Maybe you're one of them.

When you're struggling financially, it has a huge impact on your life. The commission also found that of those 27 per cent in debt, 79 per cent of them were stressed, with some literally losing sleep. Despite being employed full-time, 49 per cent of them hadn't been able to pay off a credit card some time in the previous year.

Those of us who should be doing okay can easily end up struggling in silence. We don't know how to share tips and tricks about money with each other. We don't want to admit when we're in over our heads, and we definitely don't know who to go to for help. A lot of us probably feel like we won't understand the financial jargon if we try.

That's exactly where I found myself. Treading water, worried, when I could have at least been doggy paddling. Luckily, I had one major weapon in my arsenal. I worked in journalism, a job which can be distilled down to 'find out things you didn't know before'. I also had a supportive boss and I worked for a company that liked journalists to take on extra projects.

I decided I would fix my relationship with money on company time. I just needed the right project to make it worthwhile for my employer. I hatched a plan to record a podcast, interviewing money experts about what the average person needed to do to get their finances in order. I pitched 'Cooking the Books' to the bosses as a 'mostly personal finance podcast' that would 'help idiots get their finances together'.

The bosses went for it. Little did they know that the biggest financial idiot in the room was me.

2.

Mind over money

THEY SAY THE FIRST step is accepting you have a problem. One of the first things I had to accept was that I was guilty of 'lifestyle creep'. With each of my hard-won pay rises, I immediately found something I 'needed', which soaked up my new disposable income and stopped me from using the extra money to truly get ahead.

Convincing myself stuff must have been good because it was more expensive became a pattern. A high price-tag was a shortcut that showed me something was high quality. It's easy to spend to your limit every month when you're using that kind of lazy shortcut.

I've never been paid six figures – although, note to the universe, that would be very nice – but I had managed to get to the stage where I earned a good amount of money, yet was still barely scraping by.

Part of the problem was that I'd been so broke for so long. There have been ups and downs throughout my life. I'd have a taste of the high life, followed by sudden uncertainty about whether we'd even keep a roof over our heads.

When I was a young kid, my family was reasonably wealthy – lots of toys, a nice house, all of that stuff. When I was a little older my parents got into a bitter, nasty divorce. At one point, the bank account was frozen as part of the legal games.

I remember my mum bringing home an enormous sack of carrots, because it was the cheapest thing she could buy in bulk with the little bit of cash she had. A family friend sorted us out for potatoes and onions. We had chickens, so that meant we had some eggs. It turned out Mum could be quite creative with combinations of potatoes, carrots, onions and eggs. But there's only so much creativity that can take you through several months of that. I still can't enjoy frittata.

She did her best to protect us from the stress of that time, but kids know. I would only find out later that she had only just managed to keep a roof over our heads, as well.

Then she met my stepdad, and I'd say we were comfortable through my later teens – not flash, but certainly there were no more worries about food. I got high-school jobs, first picking tomatoes, then working at a café, to get enough petrol money for a taste of freedom in rural New Zealand.

When I went to university, my savings from those high-school jobs lasted a while. I worked part-time when I could. I knew how to cut corners, surviving on carrots and hummus for surprisingly long stretches. As well as the carrots and hummus staple, there was the discovery that a can of chilli beans mixed with frozen vegetables made a surprisingly cheap, filling and tasty dinner. I spent a lot of time walking from my first job, to my second job, and then to a university lecture, so I could earn as much as possible without paying for petrol to get between them. At my flat, we stuffed bubble-wrap into the gaps in the old wooden window sills, which stopped a breeze from blowing across the room and meant we didn't feel quite so cold.

I would often cut every bill back to the bare minimum for a month just to make sure I could afford one rowdy BYO dinner out. It wasn't exactly pleasant at times, but I managed to make it work.

As the years went by, my high-school savings ran out, and higher level uni courses demanded more of my time, making it hard to hold down a part-time job. After six years of study, a casual job in journalism earning $20 an hour felt like riches.

Somehow, even as I finally got money coming in – and even after a few pay rises – I was still living pay cheque to pay cheque.

By the time I started to climb the ladder and earn more, I was like a starving person. I'd developed a mentality of 'I've earned it so I can spend it'. I stuffed myself with disposable income, spending it the moment it came into my hands, telling myself it was my reward for how hard I'd worked. Except, it turned out my 'reward' was cheating me of better and brighter things.

When I got my first real job, my eating habits changed. Carrots and hummus were finally reduced to their normal standing as a snack, and other cheap combinations – like canned chilli beans and mixed vegetables – were ditched entirely.

I don't think many people would begrudge me being able to eat real food again, but I also didn't need to replace those staples with fresh berries, takeaways at least twice a week, and regular café brunches on the weekend. I wasn't at that place where I could comfortably afford those things yet, but I was acting like I could.

My next major raise led to a change in my shopping habits. I justified this to myself by saying a job with more responsibility needs better clothes. With each pay cheque I would treat myself to a new pair of heels, an expensive skirt for the office or maybe even both. Again, work clothes can be necessary – but every single time I got paid? Come on.

If you have bad habits, a bigger income won't fix them. You'll just have those bad habits on a bigger scale.

Following my next pay rise, I decided I no longer needed to worry about dyeing my own hair. My husband was relieved of his duties as Hairdresser-in-Chief, and I started going to the salon for a professional cut and colour every three months. Never mind that they actually did a worse job of my hair than my husband had done – it was professional, so it must have been good.

Those 'small' lifestyle changes don't look so bad at first blush, do they? Maybe you look at them and think, 'Hey, what's the problem?' But a few hundred here, a few hundred there, adds up to a few thousand. I didn't have a few thousand to spare – I still wasn't even paid the average New Zealand wage. But I never looked at what was happening or checked in to my bank account, and I certainly never, ever talked to anyone about money. It was a quiet, ongoing panic, which I didn't want to think about for long – so I didn't. But it was like static in the background of my mind.

At first, it was a small voice telling me I needed to change, but when my husband called me out, a clamour started to build in the back of my head. Change was needed.

Part of the reason the dreaded lifestyle creep snuck up on me was because I'd prided myself on getting by on very little for such a long time. I'd survived six years of student living on about $250 a week. But now with a higher income, I was in a position where, if I was to suddenly lose my job, I wouldn't last two weeks.

Look, I work in the news industry. I should probably have been more prepared to survive for a while without a wage.

I'm not glorifying the years when I had nothing. They were miserable and sometimes hungry times. There's no way I want to go back to living that way just so I can pile up gold and roll around in it like Scrooge McDuck. I needed to find a middle ground where I could gain my financial independence without having to live like a monk.

If you have bad habits, a bigger income won't fix them. You'll just have those bad habits on a bigger scale. If you don't sort your head out, there's no pay rise in the world that will fix your money problems. There's no point thinking about investing, buying a house, starting a business or whatever else you think will grow your wealth, if you haven't sorted out your relationship with money.

This wasn't something I accepted willingly at first. I was still hopeful I wouldn't have to change my ways when I first met up with Hannah McQueen, whose personal finance business EnableMe was built on the idea of providing people with 'financial personal trainers'.

Like many people who sign up to work with a personal trainer, part of me was still hoping I could stick to my lazy ways, that I would be told it wasn't really my fault, and that there was some easy trick nobody had told me about. I hoped that this 'trick' I had overlooked would still let me spend everything I had without repercussions.

Unfortunately, Hannah quickly gave me a lesson in things I didn't want to hear. Her advice was that the biggest changes would come from how I handled the money I already had, not from how much was coming in.

Based on her experience, she estimates 15 per cent of the average person's income is frittered away on things they don't even enjoy. That figure doesn't even include the discretionary spending that actually brings you happiness.

Now, consider that the average person should – but doesn't – save at least 10 per cent of their income for retirement. The numbers start to align suspiciously well.

Yes, I know that's not the case for everyone, but it's the case for enough of us that I'm going to go ahead and generalise about it. If you have enough disposable income to buy a book, then we have some wriggle room to make changes.

Fifteen per cent on rubbish, things you don't need and also don't want, simply because we're not really paying attention. Those things end up costing us what we actually want – financial security, a roof over our head, a good holiday.

You only have a certain amount of money and time. In almost every job, you exchange your time for money. If you spend a week working only to blow that money on a dress you never wear, you just ticked away a week of your life for nothing. Why blow it on things you don't even care about?

For every dollar you spend mindlessly, you lose a dollar that you could have put towards travelling to Paris. That dollar could have taken you closer to starting your dream business, so you can quit the day job you don't love. You could spend that dollar taking your mum out for breakfast, because you might as well treat her while she's still around.

Before heading out the door, Hannah told me with some astonishment that most people came to her 'personal finance trainers' thinking that a pay rise would help sort their problems. As soon as they got the raise, they once again started to spend more, so ended up still stuck where they started.

Guilty. As. Charged.

When I caught up with Hannah again for this book, she said the issue was the difference between knowing and doing. Yep. At the beginning, that was definitely me. I guess at least I wasn't alone.

MANY PEOPLE KNOW THE basics – that we should spend less than we earn, and you should save, and you should buy a house. Most of us know that.

But when push comes to shove and life gets in the way, knowing and doing are two different things. Finance tends to be at the bottom of the totem pole in terms of what you'll put your effort into.

Hannah McQueen – EnableMe

WHAT REALLY HELPED TURN my mindset around was learning the difference between income and wealth. That just earning more wouldn't make me wealthy – I would simply be bringing in more and sending it straight out the door again. Meanwhile, people can become wealthy on a lower income, although it will obviously be more difficult.

Wealth is having savings to fall back on. It's having a roof over your head that you can rely on, that you've maybe even paid off. It's having investments that make you money while you have them and that you can sell in a pinch, so that you're not solely reliant on a job you could be fired from at any time.

Income is what's coming in. Wealth is any assets you have, minus your debts. Wealth is what will get you an easier life, one in which you're able to rely on yourself more and in which you have the freedom to leave situations that you don't like – bad jobs, bad relationship, boring life. Having some financial independence up your sleeve is your bargaining chip.

I finally had income, but no wealth whatsoever. I'd relaxed all of the rules as I earned more, so that income had no chance to get me the wealth I hadn't realised I needed.

I had no idea where my money was going. While I was lucky to not have any major debts, I only had about $200 saved. Investments? Those were for rich people, not normies like me.

If you went through hard times growing up maybe this problem with spending right to the limit sounds awfully familiar. That's because there's piles of research that shows scarcity actually changes the way you think. In other words, if you grew up going without, you're going to find it harder to stay in control of your money.

If you've ever gone on a diet, you'll know the feeling. Only a couple of days in and suddenly you can't remember why you're on the diet in the first place. Instead your head is crowded with thoughts of doughnuts, pasta, burgers. Before you know it, you're stuffing your face.

When you grow up with money being uncertain, it gets harder to think long-term. Your brain focuses on getting you through the short-term stress, no matter what it costs your long-term goals. It can feel like nothing matters. Why try for a better future, when it won't work? If you might not be able to pay rent this week, then it doesn't make sense to have a savings account. But what starts logically soon turns into subconscious self-sabotage. You might give in to the impulse to buy something, to give you a momentary hit of feeling good, a break from the stress, even if it means you can't pay rent that week. You might quit a stressful, low-paying job, because, hey, it's barely paying your bills anyway, so will it really be that much worse? (Yes. It will.)

Auckland University of Technology (AUT) consumer behaviour lecturer Sommer Kapitan says research shows growing up in a household where money is tight can impact your behaviour for the rest of your life. Interestingly, growing up in an unstable household can have the same affect – although the two often go hand in hand.

THIS IDEA OF GROWING up with scarce resources, or uncertainty, or lack of control over your environment . . . you might not know if you were going to get food that day, or you might not know if you will live in the same house. You can become an amazing adult, but if you grew up like that, it makes you focus on short-term gains. You never know if it will be there tomorrow, so you grab.

If you take someone and have them think about needing to repair their car, say for $1000 – for people who are broke, being reminded about a tough money decision made them perform worse on IQ tests; for people who had no worries, who could borrow money from their parents or put it on a credit card and then pay it off, they did fine on the IQ tests.

Just being cued to think about money can mess with you if you've grown up this way.

Sommer Kapitan – consumer behaviour lecturer, AUT

SOMMER SAYS PART OF dealing with this is just realising how your past will give you unhealthy impulses now. It's not that your past dictates your future – plenty of people who grew up in wealthy, stable homes can also make terrible money decisions, and vice versa – but if you're finding you regularly make unhealthy money choices, it's worth being honest with yourself about that. Personally, once I realised why I was acting this way, I was able to see just how irrational I was being. The impulses are still there, but I know what they look like and have a plan to control them.

I was only thinking short-term, because in my past short-term issues had been the important problems. Get through the now and then maybe you'll get the luxury of tomorrow. No time to plan for that tomorrow, though.

I wasn't there anymore, but my brain couldn't let go of it. I'm willing to bet a lot of people are dealing with this sort of money history. Maybe you have your own baggage that leads to a different spending pattern for you.

There's not enough research into financial behaviour for my liking, but what is around is fascinating. Research from *The Journal of Financial Therapy* (2011) found some people believe they don't deserve money; so they do things like sabotage their financial success or avoid spending money even on things that they need. They might even feel the urge to spend or give away money well beyond what they can afford, because they subconsciously want as little in their possession as possible.

The same research found that for other people money was a source of shame and secrecy. Whether they had a little or a lot, they just didn't want to talk to anyone about money. The secrecy was driven by fear, an impending sense that something was about to go wrong, whether or not there was any reason to feel that way. So they hoarded, refused to talk to anyone about money, felt anxious and never enjoyed any of the benefits or security of the money they had. What an awful way to live.

One of these might sound worryingly familiar to you or none of them might. You might do other things that you suspect aren't so healthy, which I haven't described here. Whatever your personal history is, it's worth taking the time to figure out what you're doing, why and how you're going to deal with it.

It's easy to hold yourself back when money just seems too hard. When you can't imagine getting yourself into a better financial position, you just give up and give in to every impulse that enters your head.

I was no longer struggling to eat or to keep a roof over my head. I had pulled myself towards a future where I could look after myself. Frankly, I was running out of excuses to be doing badly with my finances, and I was starting to become more aware of the traps I was allowing myself to fall into. Once you start to see what the traps look like, you can learn to sidestep them.

I was sabotaging myself. I knew I was spending money on things I wasn't even enjoying. Worse, my out-of-control cash flow was making me anxious. That low-level static was always in the back of my mind.

What made me happy? I liked having new clothes and looking good. I liked meeting friends for coffee and brunches at cafés. I liked eating well. I also knew that my husband liked eating well and I quite liked having him around, too. I wanted to do better, but I wanted to keep those parts of my life that genuinely made me happier.

It was time to experiment. It was time . . . to budget.

3.

Why save $5 on coffee when you could save $200 on rent?

I DON'T LIKE TO criticise media coverage; heck, I work in the media. I've seen how easily mistakes can be made – young reporters unaware they've repeated a common myth, people who've been talking to thought-leaders for so long, they've forgotten what the real world is like, or something phrased badly that can be taken two ways and one of those ways is horrendously offensive. Despite trying to be Zen and understanding, I still hate those articles on how much you could save if you cut out your daily coffee or the old classic of saving a house deposit by giving up avocado on toast. I have no doubt those articles are well-intentioned, but I find them endlessly patronising.

There's a time and place for cutting out the money you fritter away, believe me, but you'll do better to start with the big expenses. For most people, the big three are housing, transport and food. Changes there will have the biggest impact without you having to stress about the money involved in every little decision of the day.

Stats NZ surveyed New Zealand households between 2013 and 2016, and found that most people spend 25.6 per cent of their money on housing and household utilities. A quarter of every dollar you earn goes towards keeping a roof over your head and the lights on.

The next biggest chunk was food at 17 per cent, followed by transport at 15 per cent. Almost 60 per cent of what the average person earns goes towards the essentials of being alive and functioning. Remember, that's an average. For some, it will be far more.

It's a similar story over much of the Western world. The United States Bureau of Labor Statistics released information in 2017, which showed the average household there spent 33 per cent of their income on housing. Then transport was 16 per cent and food took 13 per cent.

Now, clearly, you need shelter and you need food. You probably need transport as well. But there's room there, if you're smart about it, to save big money automatically without having to agonise over every little cent. Contrary to what you might expect, I found that attacking these three things improved my quality of life and left me more room for the daily coffee that provides a bright spot in sometimes manic work days.

There is more than one way to skin this cat. Some people will find a cheaper place to live by being further away from work. This works well if you have good public transport, can work remotely or have a company car. Meanwhile, paying a bit more to live centrally could put your transport costs to nil if you are able to walk or bike everywhere, and thereby pay less overall.

Some people go even further by working remotely for a company based in a country with higher wages (say New Zealand or Australia) while living in a country with much lower living costs (say Cambodia or Indonesia). It's known as geoarbitrage. It's not for me as I quite like living in New Zealand, my job is flexible but still requires me to be in Auckland weekly, and I like to regularly see my family here. However, I guess I used a version of it when I moved from Wellington to Hamilton, slashing my mortgage in the process.

It's quite funny when I tell people I've moved to Hamilton. The most polite reaction from Aucklanders tends to be, 'Oh, Hamilton . . . Ummmm, why's that?'

Because it's leafy and green, big but not too big, some of my family live here, I can easily get to head office in Auckland when needed *and* I can get top quality of life for much lower dollar spend. It has all of the cafés and shops that make life easy,

Geoarbitrage Moving to live somewhere with a cheaper cost of living, to dramatically reduce your core expenses.

plenty of infrastructure, good weather and nice people. I have a far nicer house here than I did in Wellington, the right size for what we need and no bigger, and the mortgage is smaller. I have a slightly unhealthy obsession with my beautiful kitchen and even more so with my thriving vegetable garden. I've never had the space or time for one of those before. But please, if you don't believe me, don't worry about it. I don't want everyone to move here and ruin it.

I'll get into more detail on housing later, but moving here was a big win in reducing a core expense. The next issue was transport.

Throughout my entire time at university, I walked everywhere I could. I had a car, but couldn't afford to run it except to go to get groceries once a week. I imposed a limit of living within 40 minutes' walk of the university and would wear jandals for the walk, even in the depths of Wellington winter. They were cheap, took a long time to wear out, and could be chucked in my bag when I got to the destination and needed to switch to something smarter.

It turns out, when I was broke, I instinctively knew what needed to happen.

Of course, when I went into full-time work I enjoyed the freedom that came with running a car anywhere I wanted to go. So quick! Transport on demand! No weather to worry about!

Except I slowly started to stack on weight, I dreaded filling up at the pump, it was annoying trying to find a park and I always seemed to end up being the sober driver. Boo!

When we moved to Hamilton, I was adamant I wanted our home to be within an hour's walk of my work. We found a place that fitted the bill and now I walk to work through green parks, listening to podcasts or news radio. It's a relaxing way to begin and end the day, and I don't have to worry if I slack on hitting the gym. It's 100 per cent free, good for my mental health and it puts time in my schedule to stay up-to-date on world issues. I also don't have to fight for the limited parks at the office. There's literally no downside.

My husband's work is further away, but he doesn't care because he's not a big walker. He is, however, a fan of cycling. Bicycles are amazing; you pay once for a machine that costs very little to maintain, and takes you long distances quickly. The same benefits of exercise, greenery, and mental health also apply.

The biggest expenses for most people are housing, transport, and food. If you attack those you'll make a big difference for little effort.

Why would you want to spend money on fuel, a car rego, parking, if you don't have to? Every dollar I spend lugging that hunk of metal around is a dollar I can't spend on something I actually want. I don't care how much you earn; isn't it better to not have a credit card bill or be able to book flights to South America than spend on something I don't have to?

Attacking these core expenses is something that makes a big difference for little effort, so it's harder for you to fail at. It's also something that all the money geeks not only recommend, but also do themselves. When the gurus put their money where their mouth is, that's when you know the advice is good.

I don't know what a financial adviser earns, but I'm going to assume that as highly educated people who deal with money, they're not doing too badly. Over and over again, the ones I've spoken to have told me they focus on saving their discretionary money for the fun things they want to do, rather than on lazy things they don't really care about.

RIVAL WEALTH'S TIM FAIRBROTHER is one of them. He says his family can easily blow the budget on food. To keep that expense manageable, he makes sure not to waste money on café culture if he is just grabbing a quick bite during the work day.

'I would not go out of the office really to buy things. I generally go to the supermarket on a Monday and I buy salad and some snacks to keep in my drawer. I've got my tea and my hot chocolate too. For me, that's not an important thing to be spending my money on. But also, once or twice a week I'll go get lunch with a friend. That's a priority for me.

'It is different for everyone, because some people want to be out and about to meet people, for the love life or career progression. Then that's part of your plan and it really is different for everyone. That's why you need a plan. You define it, it doesn't define you.'

As you might have gathered, café culture can be a problem for me. Hey, I enjoy it, and it's often a way to catch up with friends.

I refuse to prioritise saving money over seeing people I care about, not when I have the funds available. But I do focus on reducing the cost of our main meals at home, which cuts down the overall food bill and leaves room for those times when I want to get fancy.

There are lots of ways you can cut down the food bill, depending on what works for you. Maybe go vegetarian or have smaller portions of meat. Grow some of your own food, if you're somewhere where that's possible. Sign up to one of those vege box delivery services, where you get sent a box of whatever is in season at farm-gate prices. Bulk buy when things are on special or stock up when something is in season, then store it in an energy efficient freezer. (Not a super old freezer from the 1980s – I'm afraid you'll probably spend more on power than you save on food bills.)

But the biggest thing most of us can do is cut back on food wastage.

Love Food Hate Waste has found out the average New Zealand household throws out $563 of food per year. I'm not talking egg shells and carrot tops – I'm talking perfectly good food that gets bought from the supermarket, sits in the pantry or the fridge for a while and is then thrown out. That's $500 you could spend on a coffee habit and actually get something from it.

The biggest causes of this waste are not eating leftovers or food that goes bad because we didn't store it properly. The most wasted foods are bread, potatoes, apples, chicken and bananas.

Jenny Marshall from Love Food Hate Waste told me bread was the worst for being wasted, particularly crusts and bread ends. Some people don't want to eat those bits of their bread, but it can still be turned into croutons, turned into crumbs for putting into meat loaf or crumbled on top of cheese and potatoes for extra crunch. There's always some way to eat the parts of things you don't necessarily like. Google is at your fingertips. Use it.

JENNY SAYS THE HIGHEST food wasters are usually high earners or families with children. For the families, she recommends creating an 'eat this first' shelf full of various leftovers for grazing children and teenagers. This makes sure leftovers are actually eaten and that the ingredients for the main family meal don't mysteriously go missing.

Dr Harriette Carr, deputy director of public health for the Ministry of Health, agrees that food wastage is a major problem. Their stats show the average household throws away about three kilos of food a week, and half of that is avoidable.

'One of the problems that people always say is that they prepare all of this healthy food, then the kids won't eat it and it's wasted. But if you involve the kids in preparing and cooking the food, evidence shows they're more likely to eat it.'

If the kids – or you – don't quite know where to start, Harriette recommends you check out the Healthy Kids website (www.healthykids.org.nz) for easy, free recipes. If you're staring into your fridge at a bunch of ingredients that you don't know how to put together, try the 'vegetable meal cards' you can get for free on the Health Promotion Agency's Nutrition and Activity website (www.nutritionandactivity.govt.nz). They have a bunch of information about each type of vegetable, along with

Cheesy as Meal in a Mug

This savoury dish can be a breakfast, lunch, dinner or snack – whatever you need! It's quick and easy to make, and you can easily adjust the flavourings to use up what you have.

Serves 1 — Preparation time: 5 minutes

Ingredients

2 tablespoons tomato sauce, relish, chutney, mustard or sweet chilli sauce
2 slices bread
1 egg
¼ cup milk
Pinch of salt and pepper
2 tablespoons grated cheese
2 slices ham, roughly chopped
Optional toppings: sour cream, pesto, nuts, herbs

Method

1. Spread the tomato sauce on both slices of bread, then cut into nine squares.
2. Break the egg into a mug, then add milk, salt and pepper and beat well with a fork.
3. Add the remaining ingredients in alternating stages to the mug, starting with the cheese, then ham and a few squares of bread creating layers; set aside some cheese to go on the top.
4. Press the bread pieces in the mug until it is covered with the egg and milk mixture.
5. Microwave for 1½ minutes. If it looks too soft, microwave for another 30 seconds.
6. Eat as it is or top with your choice of topping.

Cooking Tips

Any deli meat can be used for this recipe or leftover roast chicken, shredded. For a vegetarian version, try adding sweetcorn or other finely chopped vegetables.

Find more recipes like this at Love Food Hate Waste's website: www.lovefoodhatewaste.co.nz

recipes you can try with them. If the internet isn't your thing, you can also ask them to send you hard copies of the cards – again for free.

There's lots of other advice for cheaper food floating around, but you have to be careful about dishing it out. Growing a garden is great and I love it. But I love it now that I have a home that I own, which I'm not going to be moving from. Renters don't want to put a lot of love into a garden only to be kicked out by the landlord before they can harvest anything. If you work long hours or do shift work, you can be genuinely too tired to cook, never mind garden. At the beginning of my career in radio, I worked brutal shifts and learned to sleep on demand. There was no way I was going to be gardening then.

One option, though, could be planting a small herb garden. They are lower maintenance, can be transported in pots and add flavour to dishes. Sauces can be some of the more expensive items in the supermarket, and people often build up quite a collection of half-used jars. Hey, if you're able to make food at home taste great, you might avoid the temptation of even more expensive takeaways or dinners out.

If you're working shifts that mean you'll never get to those early-morning farmers' markets, then you can find cheap produce at specialty fruit and vegetable stores. The supermarket is often not the cheapest place to shop; it's simply the most convenient place because everything is there. If you split things into fruit and vegetables, the butcher and so on, then you often get a better deal overall. See what works for you.

That's housing, food and transport dealt with, but we're not quite done yet. Under housing is the sub-heading 'household bills'. The best thing about these is that if you change them once, you usually don't have to worry about it again. That's my favourite kind of saving. The automatic kind that's one and done.

Every winter, I get messages from people asking what to do about power bills. I know the pain of seeing the bills tick upwards from March onwards, trying to use as little as possible without making yourself miserable. It was particularly bad in my university days. To be fair, flatting often brings out the worst in people, particularly if none of you have much money.

I remember one cold Wellington winter, watching in open-mouthed shock as a screaming argument erupted between my flatmates over someone daring to use the hot water to wash their hands. Two flatmates literally screamed at each other in the kitchen, the first arguing that the tap was turned to hot, so someone had clearly used hot water to wash their hands. The second arguing it wasn't them and it wasn't important anyway.

It didn't seem like it was worth this level of anger to me, but on and on the screaming fight went until it fell into an icy stand-off. The rest of us steered clear – and made sure to leave the tap turned to cold in future, even if we'd just used it on hot.

Clearly, it wasn't the most adult way to deal with the problem, but I can understand why my flatmates got so mad. Each one of us was barely getting by, so every cent of power became a big deal. (For the record, I'm on Team Hot Water. Hot water and soap reduces germs better than cold water and soap. But that's admittedly a hard argument to make when money is so tight an extra $20 in bills is a big problem.)

Another of my friends flatted in Dunedin while he studied at

Otago University. He once told me a 'funny' story about how he was all bundled up in a sleeping bag, trying to read a textbook, when a particularly bold rat ran across his feet and into a hole in the wall. He was so cold and dispirited that he could only stare at it, then go back to reading. Arguably that says more about our housing stock in New Zealand, but that's a soapbox for another day.

Check out the Electricity Authority's What's My Number website (www.whatsmynumber.org.nz) or Consumer's Powerswitch (www.powerswitch.org.nz) to help work out the cheapest plan for the way your family uses electricity.

Both hot water and power are a pain because you shouldn't have to choose between bills and your health. Switching to using only cold water or actually turning off the power needs to be a last resort, but happily there are plenty of things you can do before you get to that point.

Please don't be fooled into thinking 'electricity is electricity' and that all the providers charge you around the same amount.

There's a massive difference between them, as was uncovered in the first discussion document released by the Electricity Pricing Review in September 2018.

I was horrified by the results of this review. It described a two-tier electricity sector, where one group shopped around and got good deals, while another was stung with overpriced power, late fees when they couldn't pay, and being cut off completely when the higher prices and fees spiralled out of control. The average gap between the cheapest power price and the price most people were paying was 50 per cent. A 50 per cent difference in price – just for shopping around.

Make sure you're not the person who's stung by the costs of basic necessities. You can check out the Electricity Authority's What's My Number website (www.whatsmynumber.org.nz) or Consumer's Powerswitch (www.powerswitch.org.nz) to help work out the cheapest plan for the way your family uses electricity.

If you're not in New Zealand, flex your fingers and Google 'power price comparison (whatever country you're in)'. Just about every country has consumer organisations that research this for you. You just have to find them.

Like many things, it seems almost too simple to bother recommending, but the Electricity Authority has found the average person will save $175 a year just by changing their power provider. For some people, it'll be much more. Imagine if you did that *and* made a few other changes? Why on earth wouldn't you at least check?

Each change might seem small, but add all of them together and the effect is mighty.

When I talked to EECA Energywise technical expert Christian Hoerning, he reminded me of another easy saving people often miss – the shower.

For most people, the hot water bill costs the same as or more than heating. But because it's spread more evenly over the course of the year, many people don't notice the pinch in the same way as they do for winter heating.

Christian recommends doing the shower test. Get a 10-litre bucket, turn the shower on to the settings you normally use, then run it into the bucket. It shouldn't fill up in less than a minute. If it does, you're running a stack of money down the drain.

Installing a water-saving shower head is simple, yet it could save you serious dough. They start at around $50. Water-restricting attachments are even cheaper again. Christian has worked with one family who saved $900 a year from making the switch to these attachments. You don't have to be a maths genius to work out how good that deal is.

While we're at it with the bills, check what automatic payments are going out of your bank account. There are two good reasons for this. Firstly, you'll remember what bills you're paying and be reminded to double-check whether you're getting the best deal. Your electricity, your insurance, whatever, you can usually find a better deal.

Secondly, there might be bills going out that you've forgotten. This happened to a good friend of mine when she was trying to clear their credit card debt. As she went through her statements, certain mystery payments kept cropping up. As it turned out, she had been paying $20 a month for a video streaming service she'd totally forgotten about. Who knows how long it had been going for and, needless to say, she wasn't watching any of the videos. A second mystery payment turned out to be for an Xbox gold membership – the only issue being, she didn't even have an Xbox anymore. These payments had been going out for so many months, possibly years, that she'd totally forgotten about them. It added up to several hundred dollars, at least.

I can see how this happens. We have busy lives, it's often easier to just look at the total credit card bill and pay it, but it doesn't take that long to sit down and double-check what's adding up to the money leaving your account. I'd rather spend $20 going out for breakfast than on a video streaming service I don't even know I have.

When you realise what you can gain by making a few adjustments, suddenly it feels more worthwhile. Hannah McQueen told me her clients usually liked doing things the way they'd always done them. What changed their minds was totting up how much those automatic purchases were costing them, and how that could instead go towards the life goals they really wanted to hit.

A LOT OF PEOPLE become quite set in their ways in terms of what they're prepared to give up or not, on the assumption that they're not going to achieve bigger goals anyway. If you can show them how a bigger, more audacious goal can be achieved, then people are actually open to cutting back or going without or doing things differently. They just need to know there will be a result.

Hannah McQueen – EnableMe

HANNAH SAYS, AND I heartily agree, that too much of the personal finance advice you'll find floating around will focus on helping you manage wealth that you already have. It won't help you create it in the first place. If you can change how much you're spending just to stay alive, without hurting your quality of life, then you suddenly have a lot of freed-up money you can put to work to change your situation.

You could save $563 by not wasting food, $175 by changing your power provider, $900 on hot water by buying a new shower head. You could cut your petrol bill to zero and cut the car registration as well, if you find you don't need a vehicle anymore. You can dramatically cut your rent or mortgage by making sure you live in a place that's the right size for you and maybe changing location.

All of that adds up to a few thousand a year – minimum. You can absolutely go further than this, but it's the low-hanging fruit. Pick it. No one can do this for you. You have to decide that you're sick of living pay cheque to pay cheque, that you want a future where you don't dread each bill.

Once you start seeing all these changes add up, you'll be amazed at how cutting back doesn't even feel like a hardship anymore.

4.

Moving out of vice city

SORTING THOSE CORE EXPENSES is a good way to get bang for your buck. They're big expenses, which means you have the potential to make big savings. But getting a handle on our household spending doesn't mean we can carry on ignoring our personal, day-to-day frittering away of money. I wish. But there really is no point freeing up money if you just spend it elsewhere.

In simplistic terms, I'd say there are two types of people in this world. There are spenders and there are savers.

If you leave a spender to their own devices, they will fritter away all of their money and then some. If you leave a saver to their own devices, they will hoard their cash like a dragon on a pile of gold, while wearing underwear with holes in them.

I am a spender. My husband is a saver.

This can make combining finances a little, shall we say, tricky? Money is often the foundation for every other decision, yet we end up pulling in different directions. It can also lead to a few tense conversations when we compare the personal spending side of things.

Look, us spenders aren't a lost cause or a liability. We just take a little more convincing to go against our natural instincts. We need a good reason not to spend, we need to know what's in it for us, and we need to see results.

No matter how painful it is, or how different your money personalities are, everyone I talked to said that you just had to get on the same page and figure out a budget.

Yes, you need a budget. It's that boring advice that gets trotted out all the time, but that's because it's unavoidable and it works. You can make it as simple or as complicated as you like. It's just about what works for you.

PEOPLE CAN DO IT at home just with a notebook or, if you prefer, a computer and a spreadsheet. Write down your income, then what you're spending on rent, food, power, all that stuff. Then you get an idea of where you are. It's really just keeping track of things.
Damien Hazlewood – financial mentor, Salvation Army

FINANCIAL ADVISER TIM FAIRBROTHER says if there was only one thing he could make everyone do, it would be to audit their expenses. 'It's the same thing whether you're a big corporation or a beneficiary, you have to really nail down and know where your money is going each month.

'I would say the large majority of people are disorganised on that front when they come to us. We then put stuff down on paper, in writing. We ask them, particularly couples, to be talking about their money and talking about what they want in the future. That's not necessarily money goals: usually it's personal goals, which then cost money.'

TIM SAYS THE PITFALL of this is that people would write down a plan once and then think they were done. He compares that to going to the gym once – it won't do much. You need to set up a good plan then stick with it, and regularly check that you're hitting the budget goals.

It's not like he's a hypocrite either. He still does this himself.

I SIT DOWN EVERY month, it takes me about ten minutes. I download the expenses from the credit card that month, and we go through those and we say what was food, what was power, what was phone. Then how does that compare to the budget; we've spent too much here, do we know why that was?

I'm not saying you should be scrimping and saving every single penny that you've got, but you need to know where it went. If one month we've got a whole lot in one area because we did something special with the kids maybe, we know that next month we don't have the money to do that again.

It's just reality. You can spend as much as you want, but then how are you going to pay it back again? It's easy to spend money. Harder to save money.
Tim Fairbrother – Rival Wealth

IT DEFINITELY IS HARDER to save money, but when you think about what you want from life, it's easier to find the motivation. You might think tracking your spending means you start stressing about every dollar. I've found it's almost the exact opposite – so has Tim.

'Budgeting has an image problem, but if you're living within your means, you're going to be much less stressed. You end up spending your money on things you enjoy, as opposed to spending money on unplanned things you don't care about.'

'You should track your spending' is something you'll hear a lot from financial gurus. It might be on an app, it might be a spreadsheet, it might be with a pen and paper. They'll all tell you to pick your poison and jot down a budget. There's a reason for that – it works.

It all starts by figuring out where you are now. If you hate the idea of doing that, you don't have to do it constantly, but you do have to do it.

I SUGGEST WRITING IT down. When you see it written down, it has a completely different impact. Just monitor your spending and saving

for a week. You'll be surprised at how much unintentional spending you're doing, and how much potential you have for saving.
Donna Nicolof – head of wealth and private bank, BNZ

I WANTED TO BE able to start saving for the future, to stop being a wage slave who impatiently waited for each monthly pay cheque. I wanted to buy into the sharemarket, maybe get an investment property. I wanted to be secure enough that if I ever had another job scare, it wouldn't ruin me. To make any of that happen, I needed to have money left over at the end of each month. All anyone would tell me was that the first step was a budget – and honestly, I did try.

When I broke the news to my saver husband that I was working to overhaul my relationship with money, he was quite excited. He enthusiastically sat me down and showed me the Excel spreadsheet where he had worked out his budget. He had allocated every dollar, putting it down for petrol, savings, coffee or food. There were categories and subcategories, and he even had those weird Excel equations where it will do maths for you, working out totals and subtotals. Not a single cent went unaccounted for.

His enthusiasm meant that he totally missed my boredom. I nodded and smiled wanly as he set up a similar spreadsheet for me, quizzing me about how much I wanted to spend. He emailed it to me when he was done. I never opened it again. It was so detailed, I felt overwhelmed at the mere thought of trying to stay on top of it.

After a few weeks of guiltily trying to convince myself to open the spreadsheet and stick to it, I decided to try something different. I clearly wasn't a 'track every cent' type of person. I found it overwhelming and intimidating. Fine.

I sat down by myself this time. I started with core bills, setting aside the money I needed to keep them paid. Then I decided how much I wanted to save each month, splitting the money between a savings account and an account for making investments. Bills, savings and investments first. Then spending money.

I took a look at what was left and, to be honest, I was surprised at how much there was. I decided I was allowed two major streams of spending. One chunk each week for 'social'. One chunk each week for 'vanity'.

Social could include drinks, coffees, breakfast/lunch/dinner out. Vanity included clothes, make-up, hair and all the other parts included in being a girl who likes to preen, but once that money was used up, it was used up. There was to be no going over-budget.

I'm aware that this budget was the type that some people would kill for. I know. It was a lesson in first-world problems. I didn't have any kids, my partner and I both worked decent jobs, we lived together, so were splitting the bills.

Budgeting shouldn't have been a problem for me. Yet, until then, I had dipped into overdraft every single month. Sticking to this budget was hard for me.

It helps to figure out your priorities and what makes you happy in life. Then you can figure out what fritter you're happy with, and what fritter you're not.

IF YOU'RE GOING TO buy a coffee and your lunch each day, let's say that's $20. That's $100 a week, which becomes $5000 a year. If you're earning $50,000, take off your tax and it's about $35,000, so $5000 out of that is actually a fortune.

It always depends on whether you can afford it or not, and also whether it's part of your plan.

Tim Fairbrother – Rival Wealth

YOU CAN'T ACHIEVE ANY other money goal until you start spending less than you earn. You can't buy shares with your credit card. Well, you possibly could, but you would regret it pretty fast.

It helps to figure out your priorities and what makes you happy in life. Then you can figure out what fritter you're happy with, and what fritter you're not.

To help myself stick to the new budget, I decided to make meeting people for coffee my core social activity. I might have decided on my 'social and vanity' priorities, but I still couldn't spend endlessly on them. While drinks out were fine, they tended to lead to impulsive food choices, which wasn't good for my waistline or my bank account. Brunch with friends was very enjoyable, but I often enjoyed meeting them for coffee just as much, and coffee was about a fifth of the cost of a meal.

While nothing was officially off-limits, whenever possible, I would suggest a coffee date first. It worked.

While most people have sympathy with a social-life fund, the vanity fund might seem silly to you. That's fine, everyone has different priorities, and your equivalent of a vanity fund might be gardening, homewares, car accessories or books. Replace 'vanity' with whatever silly emotional thing you don't want to give up. If you can include it in your budget in a reduced way, you're more likely to make it over the long term, and long term is what you need this to be.

Any time there's an emotional connection to something, you will try to find ways to justify still buying it. It's easier to play this mental game with yourself over little things, because you can conveniently ignore how they add up.

ADVERTISEMENTS WILL OFTEN COMMUNICATE in emotions, to try and connect to us on an emotional basis. Marketers want to bypass the rational part of us that knows we don't need a new car, we're fine with the one we've got. We tend to invest more energy in making the bigger purchasing decisions because there's more perceived risk.

Sandra Smith – marketing lecturer, University of Auckland

I STARTED AT A basic level, deciding I would stretch the vanity budget further by giving thrift shopping a crack. Honestly, I expected the rummaging to be annoying, but I was surprised at how quickly good stuff turned up. People often donate quality clothes that just don't fit them anymore, or unwanted gifts. Add to that the fact you're increasing your odds of finding unique clothes, like clothes from overseas that you can't get in New Zealand, and it's a win-win. I even dragged out an old sewing machine that hadn't been used in years and started altering things to make them perfect for me.

If ethics worry you, then the ethical bonus of second-hand shopping is huge. You've just taken a step towards stamping out sweat-shops and overflowing landfills. The apparel industry is widely acknowledged as the second worst industrial polluter after oil. Buying ethically is hard; the easiest way for most of us is to simply buy less. For the times when you can't just not buy it, second-hand comes pretty close.

This isn't to say that it was plain sailing. Oh no. Some vices had dug their claws in deep. In the beginning, I came up with every excuse under the sun for why I needed to keep allocating a lot of money to hair, make-up and clothes.

Anything that went near my skin made it particularly easy to lie to myself, telling myself I 'needed' to buy top-shelf stuff. I have horribly sensitive skin, which can break out in both eczema and acne at a moment's notice. I'd convinced myself that the only way to get around this was to buy the good stuff – even if it sent me broke.

When I decided to open my eyes, I realised that was not the case at all. Worse, I found that just a little bit of homework could get me cheapies that worked better than the expensive stuff.

First, I switched out my expensive cleanser for one that had been a favourite in high school. I was cautious at first, keeping watch for a couple of weeks for any sign of my skin going downhill. Instead, there was an improvement.

I switched out moisturiser, mascara and blush, finding with each one that I was able to find something that performed better for about a third of the price. I held off on foundation for a long time, still somehow believing the lie that expensive meant better, just in this one case. When I finally made the leap, I once again found a cheaper alternative that worked better for me.

The trick behind most of this was deceptively simple. I just decided what I wanted and put it into Google.

Allowing yourself to indulge your vices now and again will make it easier for you to manage long term. Do things less often instead of cutting them entirely, or use Google to find a cheaper way to indulge.

You're never alone in our digital era, and I soon found that I'm not the only girl who wants to have my beauty cake and eat it too. There are make-up devotees who have researched all of this for you, and you only need to read what they've written. 'Best drugstore mascara', 'drugstore long wear blush', 'drugstore bronzer for sensitive skin'. Yes, this is one instance where you want to embrace Americanisms and use 'drugstore' when you mean 'cheap'. There are lots of American girls online, and they've found the difference between the good and bad budget products.

Plenty of people have spoken out about the make-up rort, if you're willing to listen. Randy Schueller, a cosmetic chemist with decades of experience, lifts the lid on beauty myths through his website, The Beauty Brains (thebeautybrains.com). He says only 15 per cent of the cost of make-up comes down to ingredients, even for those fancy brands where you think you're paying more for those 'quality' ingredients.

It makes sense when you think about it. Lipstick can cost $40 or more, when it's just a combination of wax, oil and pigment. You're not even getting 'special' wax – Schueller says make-up price has very little relationship to quality.

What are you paying for? Packaging, marketing and brand prestige, according to Schueller. For New Zealanders and Australians, add an extra cost for the transportation and storage of make-up, because we're on the other side of the world from where most of this is produced. Even where your make-up is sold counts towards the cost, as it's considered part of the 'marketing' or 'prestige'. Sephora or Mecca are considered more prestigious than your average pharmacy.

Maybe you hope you're paying for something other than materials, like ethics or good working conditions? Price isn't a shortcut for that either. The 2019 Ethical Fashion Report put together by Tearfund, gave fancy pants Trelise Cooper an F for worker empowerment. World was barely any better, getting a D-. Meanwhile, cheap and cheerful Cotton On got an A-, as did t-shirt company AS Colour. Go figure.

I'd been lazy enough to assume that 'expensive' was a shortcut to 'better', but it turned out that those upgrades I had 'treated' myself to when I got a raise had simply been masquerading under a fake halo. The halo effect on expensive products made me overlook the most obvious drawbacks. Like, that they didn't work as well.

'You get what you pay for' doesn't hold any water with me, not any more. 'You get what you research for' is far more accurate. Five minutes online and I can pinpoint the best quality at the most reasonable price. Other people online are obsessed with this stuff. All I have to do is read what they've written.

I don't scour the internet for the cheapest knock-off blush I can find. Spending $2 for a product containing lead isn't a win for me. But I will get the best quality for the lowest price – that's called value.

Again, your vice may be different. This isn't an opportunity to laugh at silly vain ladies wasting their money – I can find you similar stats on cars, if you'd like. The underlying message is the same. Price is not a shortcut to quality. If it's not shelter, food or transport, I doubt that you 'need' it.

Retraining myself to see the difference between need and want, and treating them appropriately, gave me back a sense of control that also built up my money confidence. Gone was the guilty twinge that could follow me around for weeks, knowing I'd overspent and had nobody to blame but myself. I was not only changing my mindset, I was changing my relationship with money. I was learning I didn't have to fear it. I didn't have to stay in a zone of foggy avoidance, not looking at the bills coming in or the money left in my account, because of the fear it was all going wrong.

Sure, my generous budget that included coffee with friends and saw thrift shopping as cutting back might sound silly. As my money journey has continued I've seen the rewards and found cutting back easier, so the budget has become stricter. But this training budget helped me get into the mindset of staying within my limits, while not having to feel deprived. It also showed me I had plenty of money for the things I wanted to do when I cut out the things I didn't care about in the first place. Like I say, many of us feel like we don't have enough money, when the real problem is that we're not being smart in how we use the money we have.

As I got a handle on things, I started to talk to friends more openly about money. In one of those conversations, I was given one of the best money tips I've ever heard. A friend told me to rotate what I cut back on each month, then I would never feel deprived overall.

One month, maybe you won't go out for after-work drinks. The next month, your social life is resuscitated, but you're not buying any clothes. The next month, you can buy those jeans you want, but you're going to avoid using your car and walk everywhere that you can.

It worked. Each time I cut something completely for a month, it's a reminder that I'll pay for the things I want in my life and nothing more.

I believe that, just like a diet, if you try to cut everything at once you will only make yourself miserable and give up. If you look at why you enjoy the things that you enjoy and think about how to enjoy that more sustainably, there is often a cheaper way to go about it.

All of this applies only to genuine vices; indulgences that you could do without, but don't want to, because you enjoy them. It's not just mindless spending, but on cheaper stuff.

Otherwise, underneath the vice trap lies a new trap. You switched your consumption to cheaper products? Good, good. But keep in mind that cheap doesn't mean good value. At a certain point, you'll also need to learn the discipline of just buying less stuff.

It's astonishing how much money we can waste on things we neither need nor want. Keep a diary of everything you spend and then how much you either enjoyed or used that thing. The results will surprise you. Those are the things you cut entirely. If a daily barista coffee is the bright spot of your day and you can afford it, don't cut it. If you mindlessly buy lunch and shove it down without tasting it, it's time to start bringing something cheaper from home.

Keep a diary of everything you spend and then how much you either enjoyed or used that thing. The results will surprise you.

The thing is, you can switch from 'expensive means good' to 'cheap means good', and keep right on spending. But sales and bargains play into a nasty bit of human psychology. If you get something that was $80 and is now $20, you're not saving $60. You're spending $20. It all adds up. If you buy rubbish you don't need, it doesn't matter how good the bargain was. That's why a lot of marketing and retail tricks are built on trying to get you to make an immediate decision.

EVERY TIME YOU SEE a sale it creates a feeling of scarcity; limited time only, must buy now, all of that. It's pushing all of these triggers that make you want that immediate reward, which is impulse buying.

Especially in New Zealand, we like to be seen as smart shoppers, so if you get a compliment, the first response tends to be 'thanks, I got it 30 per cent off'. We're proud to get a deal. And it's true that we should hunt those out, but retailers know feeling smart and competent is something shoppers desire. If you didn't need that bag at all, then they've won. You spent money you didn't need to spend.

They'll also try to build in the things that could surprise and delight you. Christmas is really big for nostalgia, that's a powerful emotional trigger. By playing Bing Crosby and putting up mistletoe, they're sending me back to all of these really happy memories. And if they can play on that, dropping in other related items nearby that you're surprised by, they'll capture your attention and get you to spend your dollars there.

Sommer Kapitan – AUT

SOMMER SAYS THAT PEOPLE will make fun of the lines and crowds for things like the Black Friday sales, but that those sales tap into a feeling that buying a certain item will make you belong; and that today will be the only day you can afford to join that exclusive club. You're not just someone who watches TV, you're someone who has a 60-inch screen and surround-sound speakers. You're a connoisseur.

As my dad used to say: 'If you don't think they're out to get you, you haven't been paying attention.'

As always, part of winning this little game comes by knowing that you're playing it in the first place. Then there are a few other tactics you can try out to strengthen your willpower.

I know that a money diary sounds like it's too simple to do much, but try it. Write down everything you spend in a week. Next to each entry, write down how happy that made you. Not just in the moment either; a moment of impulse happiness followed by five days of guilt and regret needs to be recorded in the diary.

Take a beat when the urge for an impulse purchase comes up. Ask yourself if this thing will make you happy, or if you're buying out of boredom or habit. Ask yourself if you need it and be honest with your answer.

Sometimes a walk around the block can be enough to get control of yourself and realise that you not only don't need it, you actually don't even want it. Some people even live by the rule that they have to wait two weeks before buying anything, finding that few things survive the cooling-off period.

Sommer Kapitan says she also grew up in a home where money was tight and the living situation a little unstable. Like me, she's more prone to impulse buying than many people. She got a handle on it by focusing on bigger goals, by reminding herself that if she puts back the cutesy pool float, she can keep putting money towards the holiday with her husband and kids. She reckons that every time she's done this successfully, it was much easier the next time.

To be honest, the biggest difference came when I just decided to try. What really matters is setting up whatever kind of budget you can stick to and that stops you spending more than you have. What works for one person won't work for another, because overspending, or 'undisciplined spending' as some smart people call it, is all relative to how much money you have coming in.

Deep down we all know this. To quote the famous Charles Dickens character, Mr Micawber: 'Annual income twenty pounds, annual expenditure nineteen, result happiness. Annual income twenty pounds, annual expenditure twenty pounds and six, result misery.'

It's not just me and Charles Dickens who found that budgeting can actually make you happier. That is, if you do it right.

The Commission for Financial Capability released a survey on people's attitudes to debt in late 2017. Two of the results really stood out to me.

The first was that a third of people responded saying they worked hard, so felt they deserved to spend their money. I can understand that, up to a point. I think we've all had a day where the only cure for workplace drama is to nip down to the pub. But then half of the people surveyed also answered that they had debt and it worried them.

You 'deserving' to spend your money can actually lead you into spending that you can't afford. That stuff won't bring you happiness; it will just backfire and stress you out.

To make it easier to track my success (or failure), I streamlined my bank accounts. Having obvious pots of money made it easier to keep an eye on things while still avoiding the dreaded Excel spreadsheet. I set up a couple of extra bank accounts, so that I had four in total. The bank was happy to organise it for me and I made sure that three of the four were only accessible through online banking, so I could save on fees. These were only my accounts. We set up others for our joint bills. But it gives you an idea of how I was thinking.

MY MAIN SAVINGS ACCOUNT was only to be touched in case of emergency or an unexpected bill. My save to spend account took away my excuse to dip into my main savings account when I wanted to pay for life's bigger, fun expenses like booking a holiday.

My mortgage account came about thanks to a small pay rise of $20 a week. Previously this would have been soaked up by a small increase in fritter, probably socialising. But instead I saved it to go onto the mortgage; you don't miss what you never had. More on this and compound interest later, but unbelievably, this tiny extra knocked years off the mortgage. The idea of getting the house paid off so much faster turned out to be an amazing motivator. Before long, the savings accounts started to look pretty healthy. The more I flexed the savings muscle, the more the rewards started to come and the stronger I became mentally.

Personal accounts

Account one:
my regular bank account for bills and spending money

Account two:
my main savings account, which had an automatic payment go into it with each pay

Account three:
my 'save to spend' account, which was for saving for expensive things

Account four:
my mortgage account, which was where I put a $20 a week pay rise I'd been given

Joint accounts

Account one:
household bills and spending

Account two:
emergency savings account

Account three:
savings for household maintenance

Account four:
savings for feline healthcare (why do they always get sick at midnight and need the after-hours vet?)

Others to consider

Donations:
if you like to donate money to charity, include in your budget

Gifts:
plan for Christmas and birthdays by including a regular amount from your budget

While I wasn't a spreadsheets kind of person, I could be a broad overview type of person. I could work within a total figure as long as I had a goal in mind and strategies to remind myself that short-term weakness meant long-term unhappiness.

What's interesting is that with every step on this journey, I found it easier to make the much bigger steps. It was the first small reductions in my budget that were the hardest, to create those first small savings. The longer I stuck with any change, the easier it became, especially when the rewards came.

The rewards came much faster than I expected, as well. Particularly the reward of less stress. That was almost instant.

You don't have to give up everything, but you should give up all the things you won't miss, then find smarter ways to indulge your vices.

5.

You don't look successful, you look stupid

ONE PLACE I'VE LUCKILY avoided problems is with status symbols. Maybe it's the flip side of growing up with a lot of resources, then a little, then some. I just don't feel like I tell the world about myself through the expensive things that I have. Yet many people do, and it's a really good way to accumulate dumb debt. The worst part is that it usually backfires and tells the world something that you never meant to say.

There are all sorts of status symbols that suck people in. Cars are kryptonite for some. Designer clothes. Fancy homewares. Prestige-brand anything. It's the emotional connection to this stuff that trips people up. I once had someone tell me about a car they'd bought with an enormous loan: 'I need it. I need to look successful. It will help me in my job.'

Rubbish. People will use this 'looking successful' excuse for all sorts of things that they want, but can't afford. It's a lie you tell yourself in order to make a big emotional purchase you know you can't actually justify. If you want it, it makes you happy *and* you can afford it, well, that's one thing. If you're buying it because of what you think other people think, then why on earth would you bother?

Honestly, after gambling, showing off to other people is one of the silliest ways to spend money. Almost nobody cares – we're a bit busy worrying about our own lives. Not only will you not look successful to many people, expensive bells and whistles can actually backfire when it comes to what other people think of you.

I like to lurk on Sharetrader, an online forum for those who invest in shares. (Yes, I will get to investing once I'm done waxing lyrical about budgeting. Everything in due course.) It's an interesting way to pick up on market chatter from people who are smarter than me and have more insider access than I do.

I was once reading a discussion about a start-up company, which shall remain nameless. The company had created an app that some people with more money and more appetite for risk than me were considering investing in. There was no way I could afford it, but it was an interesting debate to lurk on.

Particularly after one guy spoke up. He told the group he'd actually visited the start-up's office. He thought they were on to a good thing, that the market was ready for their idea and that they had the expertise to pull it off. Despite this, he wasn't going to invest.

Why? Because outside the office, the staff had parked up their Mercedes, Audi and even Ferrari cars.

This was a sign to him that they didn't know how to manage expenses; that they would make dumb financial decisions; that their attitude to money could eventually kill their idea, despite everything else looking good. The issue he was picking up on is that a car you can't afford is the ultimate decision in dumb debt. It's different from, say, a house.

Debt doesn't have to be your enemy, but there's a big difference between smart and dumb debt. Use that difference to your advantage.

A house's value (hopefully) goes up over time. The house will (hopefully) still be there in 30 years when you have (hopefully) paid it off, and can live in it mortgage free through your retirement. You can also use it as collateral for other investments if you want to get fancy. A bank sees that you have a valuable asset like a house, and they let you borrow money against it, leveraging your home to buy an investment property or start your own business. That's smart debt. You still want to pay it off as quickly as possible, but you shouldn't feel too bad about taking on a mortgage as long as you can afford the repayments.

A car, however, continually drops in value. A 2017 survey by Carspring found that New Zealand cars depreciate faster than those anywhere else. On average, our cars lose 54 per cent of their value after being driven just 56,000 kilometres. If you live somewhere else in the world, I'm afraid your car has still lost value by the time you drive it out of the car yard. It's just New Zealand cars are extra speedy about it.

The loans you take out to buy a car usually have a high interest rate, maybe around 15 per cent or so. That interest rate means the loan will continue to grow while your car value continues to drop. By the time you pay it off, your car may be getting old, and you might think you 'need' a new one, so you stay in an expensive debt cycle.

There is an argument that spending more gets you a higher quality car, but only up to a certain level. After that, you're buying a brand and marketing.

Cade Wilson, the motoring adviser for AA (the Automobile Association), kindly gave me some car-buying tips. As a general rule of thumb, most cars are mechanically reliable 0–10 years. If a car is aged from 10–20 years, you can get it cheaper, but you might have more repairs and maintenance to carry out. Older than 20 years and you get into bigger mechanical problems more often. Although, of course, if you know how to fix them yourself, that's no problem.

Leveraging Using debt to make an investment. Often means using the value of your house to borrow more money from the bank, to then invest in something like an investment property or starting a business.

Cade also recommends you spend $20 on a vehicle history check, which could save you thousands. The report will tell you if the car was imported with damage, and also if someone else has taken out a loan against a car at some point. You don't want it to be repossessed by a debt collector after you've bought it. Getting a pre-purchase inspection done is a good idea, rather than relying on the Warrant of Fitness to tell you if a car is in good nick. The WOF is just a safety check, and it doesn't give you any information on important things like the engine condition or transmission issues. You really don't want a car with transmission issues. They can cost more than the entire car to fix.

That's it. That's all the stuff you need to worry about – safety, reliability, how much it costs you now and how much it will cost you later. The tips Cade gave me are freely available online. Substitute 'car' for whatever 'investment purchase' you're considering, and do some research through Google for what you need to know before you buy. It's all at your fingertips – and it might save you thousands.

For once, I have happily avoided an emotional connection when it comes to buying a car. Everyone has different things that set them off, and this just isn't one of those things for me. When I needed to buy a new car a few years back, I realised a focus on safety and reliability wasn't the attitude the salespeople expected me to have. Not at all.

We were changing from a one-car household to having two cars, because our work schedules changed and we couldn't carpool anymore. Being a pair of shift workers in a big city like Auckland was annoying; nope, you can't catch a bus at 3.30am.

I wanted the new car to use very little petrol, to have cheap parts available for any repairs and to have a good safety record. A bit of searching online and I eventually hit on the Mazda Demio. My research made it clear I wanted the newer version, which had better safety features. At that point, that meant a 2009 version or newer.

As I started touring the used car yards, seeing what was available, I met unexpected resistance to my clear requests.

'A Demio? Here's a beautiful little number, 2007, very few miles. Yellow, a lovely bright colour for a lovely young lady.'

'It needs to be 2009 or newer, sorry.'

'No problem! Here's one from 2008. And it's purple.'

I stared at him. Then I left. Only to have the exact situation repeat at three more car yards.

Note to car salesman: please stop assuming ladies are dummies who can't do research on cars and only care what colour the paint is. It's a great way to make sure they leave – fast.

Eventually I found a direct-import company selling a 2010 Demio. It was a bit cheaper than other car yards because it was straight in from Japan. The radio was still tuned to Japanese frequencies and there was a weird bit of gadgetry that was apparently used for going through Japanese toll booths.

I took it to a mechanic, checked there was nothing actually wrong with it and got the all-clear. Then I took it back to the car yard and pulled out my trump card.

'Hmm, I'm just not sure I can afford it. If anything changes on price, this is my number, okay?'

He called me the next morning with a great offer. I hmmed and hawed, then asked for slightly below that. He agreed. When

I called to get it insured, the guy noted with surprise that I'd beaten the market price by about $2000. I've never been so damn smug.

Actually, I'm smug quite often. It's a personality flaw. But that was still top five.

Of course, the other problem with cars is that they can cost quite a bit – even the cheap ones. Sometimes you get a new job, which means you need a car ASAP, but you don't have any savings. I'm not judging anyone for needing a loan for a car. Not everyone is in the position to buy without debt, and sometimes you need it for that job that will improve your lot in life. Of course, it's better to avoid the car and use a bike, walk, carpool or take public transport instead. But for the times when that's genuinely not possible, you can at least make the loan as small as possible.

A good rule of thumb, given to me by Hannah McQueen from EnableMe, is to make sure you can pay off the car loan within three years. Can't pay it off within three years? Then maybe you can't afford that particular car.

Yes, the argument that you need to spend well out of your budget just to look good to other people is ridiculous, and cars are just the example I've chosen. But the real problem is looking for status symbols to impress people who aren't paying attention to you and don't care what you have.

How about some lovely diamond jewellery? The type that sparkles in the sun, can be passed down to your children or sold if you ever hit really tough times?

Well, it's probably worthless. Most jewellers don't like to buy back diamonds, and if you can convince them to do it at all, it will probably be for a fraction of what you paid for them.

An infamous 1982 investigation by Edward Jay Epstein for *The Atlantic* magazine detailed several studies where this happened. Epstein describes a 1976 case when the Dutch Consumer Association tried to sell a perfect one carat diamond to 20 leading Amsterdam dealers, eight months after first buying it. Of those jewellers, 19 refused to buy it and the twentieth offered a pittance compared to the purchase price. In another case, the London-based consumer magazine *Money Which?* repeatedly tested diamond resales through the 1970s, sometimes being offered less than half of what they had paid for the gems.

Most jewellery is just another depreciating asset, or, in plain language, something you will pay a lot for in the store, which loses value the moment you walk out with it. There are lots of these types of things around, things that plenty of people will try to convince you are an 'investment' – in yourself, your happiness, your future. Don't fall for it.

It's an easy trap to think a certain thing would make you happier. Yet it almost always fails to do so.

MONEY, IN OUR SOCIETY, is a symbol of our worth – that we're smart, can invest, can afford these things. If you're able to display it in fashion or a big screen TV, it says that you're doing well in the system. But when you privilege the immediate, you will eventually lose out on what you need in the long term.

Most people, if you asked them, would not say that they're doing it for status. But there's the idea that you buy something, and you buy the best version of it, because you're the type of person who buys the best. Most people wouldn't be conscious of that, but it is an underlying motive.

It's buried deep within us and tied so deeply into our own self-esteem.

Sommer Kapitan – AUT

IT'S A SIMPLE SHORTCUT to think that money will make you happy, and if you can just get more of it, you'll be happier. Of course, having more money means you can buy more things, so those things must surely make you happier as well. But having more stuff often means just more maintenance, more bills to pay, more work to pay for all of that. Poverty is clearly extremely stressful, but there's also a point at which more money will also only make you miserable.

A 2018 study published in *Nature Human Behaviour* found that if you earn more than US$75,000 a year (about NZ$110,000), you become less happy. To me, that looks like a stunning amount of money. You could go on holiday all the time, have a gorgeous house, go to cafés for breakfast, lunch and dinner. What's there to be unhappy about?

Comparison. The thief of all joy. Because once you earn more than that, people start to fixate on social comparisons and building up material things that bring them no happiness. In fact, according to a 2002 study in the *Journal of Economic Psychology*, the more you fixate on material things and financial success, the more likely you are to become unhappy.

Money can give you options, buy you freedom, get you closer to goals, absolutely. But if you're focused on money for the sake of it, or on building up a pile of 'stuff' without questioning why, then you will actually have less happiness, more anxiety and possibly even physical symptoms of stress. Go figure.

If any of your 'stuff' ties into how you think of yourself, or triggers strong emotions like anxiety, it's probably a status symbol. You don't need things to tell you who you are. Enjoy them, sure, when you can afford them. But *you* control things. The things and the emotional need for things shouldn't control you.

The worst of the lot is the status symbol that people buy, but never even use. A quick hit of buying something that ties into who you would like to be, that makes you feel better in the moment, only to never be used.

The more you fixate on material things and financial success, the more likely you are to become unhappy.

People will build up piles of stuff, impulse purchases that they felt would be the key to happiness in the moment. This has us drowning in stuff we've bought with hard-earned cash, but that we don't need, don't want and don't enjoy.

While bigger houses are often a status symbol in themselves, we also buy them to hold all this extra stuff. I'm talking *much* bigger houses – according to Stats NZ, between 1970 and 2016, the average size of a New Zealand house ballooned out by 60 per cent. In the US, it's even worse. Their national statistics show that, over the same time period, the average house size has nearly doubled. Meanwhile the storage business is booming. One IbisWorld industry report in Australia showed the storage industry making increasing profits over the last five years, predicted even more for the next five, and credited the trend to households needing places to store extra furniture and cars. Look, if you're not even using it, why on earth do you have it?

Here's a thought; how about we only have stuff we need, use and enjoy. Get rid of the emotional impulse buys, the purchasing of things to show off to people who aren't paying attention, clear out the storage unit full of stuff you're paying to have but never use or even see. Clear out the spare bedroom's wardrobe and don't refill it. Heck, you might even find you no longer need such a big house. Imagine how much you could save then.

Once you admit these emotional crutches to yourself – and let go of them – that's when you can start to make the real gains. The ones that improve your stability, your happiness, yes your self-esteem. Not in the temporary ways, with the short boost followed by a sharp drop, but for real, this time.

Hannah McQueen says if she only had one thing she could tell people, it is that most of us have the ability to dramatically change our current situation.

YOUR DEFAULT, IN TERMS of what you've been doing and want to keep doing, is so different from your potential. For many people, there's a lot of room to move, you just can't see the angles because you're too close to yourself. People call it early and assume that their default is their future.

It's not true. Well, it is true if you're not prepared to do anything about it. But if you understand the detail, you can make some strategies to get to your goal. Then you will want to be different because the outcome is different to what you thought was possible.

Hannah McQueen – EnableMe

THOSE WHO'VE LISTENED TO my podcast will know I have a British accent. That's because I was born and lived in England until I was eight. England can be a little obsessed with class and improving your station, so my mum had a hilarious experience when she tried to attain her own status symbol.

When she was younger (well before I was on the scene) she would walk past Harrods, the fancy department store. It had a café full of overpriced treats where you had to pay just to go in. For a long time, she felt that if she could have a strawberry tart in Harrods, she would have made it.

She was just starting out in her career, so was fairly broke. Eventually, she saved up, and went in with a friend. They bought a strawberry tart to split and a black coffee each. They sat in the window of Harrods, feeling posh, accomplished. Until they heard a haughty voice behind them. 'Oh my dear, I wouldn't be seen *dead* having strawberries without champagne.'

The pair of them burst out laughing. They still hadn't made it.

You'll never be able to buy the status symbol that truly shows how successful you are. There will always be someone the next level up, looking down at you. If you play this game forever, your status symbols will just get bigger and bigger, and you'll always want what the people above you have, while never appreciating what you've got.

You could choose to opt out entirely. Because who can be bothered playing a game that only wins approval from dickheads? I couldn't care less what that type of person thinks of me.

Stop being manipulated into making emotional choices that you think reflect your worth as a person. Maybe yours isn't a car or jewellery. Maybe it's getting a designer pet, or buying a house in a certain suburb even if it's not the most convenient place for you to live. Pay attention to yourself and the emotions that certain things are tapping into. Take back the control, to only give away your money when it's genuinely the right call for you.

Seven years later, my little Demio still runs like a dream. The person who told me they needed the more expensive car to 'look successful' at work has since had two major repairs done on that car, and then 'upgraded' to yet another expensive lemon.

As for looking more successful . . . well, Dr Thomas Stanley has researched millionaire habits for years, even writing books about them for those of us who feel curious. In his book *Stop Acting Rich*, he looked at what types of cars people drove and how wealthy they were. His result for the most popular car brand among millionaires? A Toyota. Because of the brand's reliability.

Anyway, my Demio looks super cute. And it's very easy to park.

6.

Be young and carefree, just not with your money

TO SOME PEOPLE, THIS will sound like too much sacrifice for someone my age. I started this journey in my late twenties. Who in their twenties needs to worry about budgeting, getting their money mindset right or working towards financial independence with investments? Really, aren't your twenties the time to be young and dumb?

It's the time to take that trip, even if it means putting it on a credit card. It's the time to bounce between jobs; careers are for later. It's the time to ignore the future and live in the now, while you're young enough to enjoy it.

Actually, my only regret is that I didn't start this money mission in my early twenties.

For one thing, you don't turn 30 and suddenly become an invalid who can't travel. You also don't waltz into a highly paid management job that lets you provide for a family, after years of bouncing between casual gigs.

Tomorrow comes around quicker than you expect, and you'll still be you, and you'll still want to do fun things. Whether or not you can depends on what you do today.

I want to live for today *and* tomorrow. I want to have fun now *and* when I'm old. Why can't I have it all? There's no reason why you can't – as long as you have a strategy.

There's also one big, crucial reason why you should start looking after your money as young as possible. That's because when you're young is the best time to make the most money with the least effort. You can't make up for lost time when you're older. Compound interest will no longer be working as hard for you.

Compound interest are the two little words that will light up the face of most personal finance nerds, or lead to a knowing smile from someone who works in the industry. Einstein famously called it the eighth wonder of the world, and I'm not going to disagree with that guy. It stops you having to work for every dollar yourself. With a bit of time on your hands, your money grows without you having to do anything. The trick is you need quite a bit of time – as in, decades.

Compound interest A beautiful way to make money without trying. Any interest or investment profits go back into the pot and start earning you money. Before you know it, you're earning profit on profit.

That doesn't mean you should give up if you're older. It's simply that time is the biggest and best ingredient for growing your money. If you stash away $10 in your twenties, it will do far more for you than $20 in your forties.

Like a rolling money snowball, if you put that $10 somewhere smart, it can start earning you money. Every bit of money it earns you will then also get to work to earn you even more money, and as your pot of money grows it keeps giving you bigger and bigger returns. Time gives your money snowball a longer space to roll and keep picking up more money, therefore getting a lot bigger for less effort.

Saving $10 a week from the age of 20

THE COMMISSION FOR FINANCIAL CAPABILITY has run the numbers, looking at what happens if you save just $10 a week starting from when you turn 20. With compound interest, by the time you hit 40, that $10 a week becomes over $13,000. By 60, it's $35,480, and 40 per cent of that is interest – free money. Beautiful, easy, compound interest. But if you start just 10 years later, you'll miss out on about half of that free money.

Starting saving at 20 versus 30

- Saving $10 a week from the age of 20, the end result at 60 is $35,480 – $14,680 of that is compound interest. Close to half of it.

+ Saving $10 a week from the age of 30, the end result at 60 is $23,110 – $7,510 of that is compound interest. Just under a third.

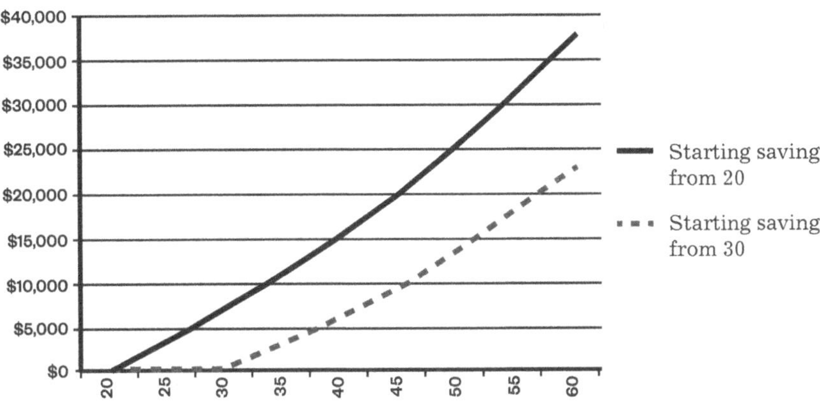

Data courtesy of Sorted (sorted.org.nz)

It's easy to underestimate compound interest, but it becomes a powerful money-making machine when given enough time.

IN THE SHORT TERM, you're looking at differences in returns that don't seem very big. To the lay person, if you look at different returns, even between 5 and 8 per cent, you might think 'Oh, three percentage points, that's not such a big deal, surely?'

But in the finance world, the difference between 5 and 8 per cent is huge. Finance people talk in basis points, which is a hundredth of

a per cent, because these differences can become so big over time. Over a decade it's a huge difference, because that interest snowballs up and supercharges your wealth.
Tom Hartmann – personal finance editor, The Commission for Financial Capability (CFFC)

EXCEPT UNFORTUNATELY, ACCORDING TO CFFC research from 2013, only 32 per cent of New Zealanders understand what compound interest is. So if this is all new to you, you're far from alone. We need to fix that though, because it's the easiest and laziest way to earn money. All you need is time and a bit of self-control.

Have you got a KiwiSaver or some other retirement fund? Have you ever looked at the way the balance usually rockets higher each year, even if you don't put anything extra in? That's compound interest. It's your best friend. That's why the earlier you get started, the more rewards you'll get, for the least pain.

AUT associate professor of finance Aaron Gilbert says he often asks his new students if they've started investing. The result is usually a small show of hands; particularly depressing considering they're students who have signed up to study finance. Even a little bit from high-school jobs could turn into a lot of money, just by being given the time to compound.

THE WHOLE THING IS, start early, contribute frequently, give it as much time to compound as you can. From an academic perspective, that's how you build wealth in the long term.

It's not a quick solution, you won't be rich overnight. Anything that will tell you otherwise is probably not something you want to touch with a ten-foot pole. But you will be rich, if you give it time. Discipline and starting early is what builds wealth.

Aaron Gilbert – associate professor of finance, AUT

KARL ARNS IS SIMILARLY passionate about getting started when you're young – and he should know. When I first met him he was a 25-year-old authorised financial adviser and an institutional commodities dealer for OMF. He was 26 by the time I talked to him again for this book, and he was still making the rest of us look like shocking underachievers by comparison. He's making compound interest his best friend to keep his options open in life.

HAVING SOME MONEY WHEN you're young and investing those returns so they can compound for you, it really does make the world of difference. Time is everything, it's the most precious commodity we have, much more so than money.

The general rule of thumb is that, over a long timeframe, returns average about 7 per cent in the stock market. On that basis, every ten years, your money doubles.

So you get exponential growth, and if you start saving ten years later than the start of your career, then you're basically retiring with half of what you would have had otherwise. So you're talking about doubling your wealth, just by starting ten years earlier.

Karl Arns – institutional commodities dealer, OMF

THIS DOESN'T MEAN THAT you give up if you're a late bloomer; after all, 10 years from now will be an even worse time to start. Nobody has a time machine to go back and start earlier, but we can start today.

Your twenties, thirties and even forties are the major compounding years of your life – the time when you can put in the effort to earning money, put that money somewhere smart and get the most reward from it.

It doesn't matter where you're starting from, or how little spare cash you have to work with. Tell me about it; I'm a journalist, I graduated with a tonne of student debt, walked into a low-paying job and then had to survive paying my bills in Auckland in the midst of a housing crisis. I'm not saying it's easy. But nothing that's worth having is ever easy. What matters is making the difference that you can, with what you have now.

I DIDN'T START WORKING with any savings behind me or anything, so maybe I'm not the best example. I came out of university with a student loan, had to relocate to Auckland for work and had a couple of thousand in credit card debt.

Ultimately, you need to follow a well-worn path. The first thing is, don't take on a lot of debt. It's obvious and it's boring, but the worst thing you can do to your finances is borrow money. There are exceptions, like productive assets or things that are absolutely necessary to support your income, but stuff like borrowing twenty grand to buy a car you don't need is never a good idea in my book.

Once you've got debt paid off, it's saving – saving as much as you can, as early as you can and then investing it where you can. Even if saving feels pointless, you can't afford a house deposit, there are alternatives. Things like sharemarket investing, index funds, you can't go wrong with KiwiSaver. There are things out there that you don't need huge sums of money for, and every little bit you save is going to make a difference.

For now, I'm choosing less travel and more savings, which is a trade-off based on my own long-term desires. I want to be able to have options. If you save hard enough and long enough then you can retire that much sooner. I want choices further down the line.

There's no benefit to feeling hopeless and spending an extra thousand dollars on a holiday or something, because you can't afford a house deposit. That's just the wrong way to look at things.

Karl Arns – OMF

EVEN IF YOU ONLY have $20 spare a week, that money can be put to work. When I first started investing in shares, I was buying $100 of shares after each monthly pay. That was a lot to me at the time and still might sound like a lot to you now.

After a year had ticked by, I had $1400 in shares. I'd put in $1200, then some of the shares increased in value and others had paid out dividends that I'd promptly used to buy more shares. It built up quickly.

Shares Shares are a unit of ownership in a particular company or financial asset. You buy a piece of that company, your share of it.

Dividends A cash payout to people who own a share in a company. It normally comes from that company's profits.

Maybe what you can afford right now is $10 a week. Do it.

Part of the problem with 'start young' is that you're just at the beginning of your career. You probably aren't earning much; I certainly wasn't. There's not a lot left over after paying your bills. But even that little bit can do a lot later. Just do what you can.

The Commission for Financial Capability's personal finance editor Tom Hartmann says your twenties and thirties are a powerful time to take control of your money, as long as you're kind to yourself about your own situation. 'They say that your twenties are about learning, and your thirties about earning. Now if you can start that earning part a little earlier, you'll clearly get a better result. The question is just, how much can you do with what you're paid? If you can take advantage of compounding particularly before you start a family, which is a very expensive enterprise, I'd really support someone in that.'

I love that phrase from Tom; he's a lovely man, and you can see it there. That's what this is about. Nobody is telling you what you must or mustn't do, but we're trying to support each other to make the best choices for each of us.

Part of it for me was forcing myself to make little changes that felt like they were going nowhere, but that changed my mindset. Those little changes add up to big things, sure, but they also push you into a mindset where you're conscious of your money, where it's going and what opportunities you're looking for next.

You get yourself ready for bigger and better things, and truly, those bigger and better things start to happen. I don't mean some nonsense like 'the secret', where the universe gives back the vibes you put out there. Don't wait for magic to save you, please.

What I mean is that when you're alert and ready, you can spring onto opportunities when they show up. Luck happens, and you'll get far more mileage out of that luck if you're prepared for it.

Little changes, the low-hanging fruit, soon added up to me being able to save hundreds each month. I set up auto-payments, so that the day after I was paid, one chunk of cash went into a savings account, one chunk went into an account for extra mortgage payments and one went into a shares trading account. As I got better at this game, I increased the amount of each of the auto-payments. Just like the automatic nature of KiwiSaver, or even tax, means that you don't miss the money you don't see, I didn't miss that money automatically going into my savings. The pain of remembering to save and invest was removed.

Set up an automatic payment to go into a savings account the day after you are paid – you don't miss money you don't see.

Before I knew it, I had a couple of thousand dollars in my emergency fund. Suddenly, I actually *was* young and carefree. Because when my cat got into a fight and had to go to the vet, I just took her. And paid for it. And everything was fine. When my black work pants developed a hole in the crotch, I just nipped into a shop on the way home and bought a new pair. No stress. No problem. Just money set aside to deal with problems when they came up.

Being a carefree idiot with my money had created stress everywhere. It turned out, keeping an eye on my money meant I could be carefree with everything else.

Of course, if you're a bit older and reading this, it's no reason to give up hope. As the saying goes: The best time to start was 10 years ago. The second best time is today.

The younger you can start, the easier it will be. You're younger today than you will be tomorrow, so get a wriggle on.

7.

Get rid of debt that will drown you

IT'S HARD NOT TO sound judgemental when talking about things like status symbols or the need to start young when planning your money journey. It's not actually judgement of anyone who falls into these traps. It's frustration that greedy companies are winning. With nothing more than a sparkly veneer and some shady, emotive marketing, they take people's hard-earned cash off them.

I get that money is hard, life is hard and we're all just people juggling our different situations. But just because we're all different doesn't mean I can skip over these things in case they don't apply to someone. They do apply, in some form, to the majority of us. Being honest and changing the things that we can are important parts of changing your relationship with money to be healthier.

Every industry is trying to persuade you to spend more money than you have. Trying to convince you that the right car, the right outfit, the right house will be what finally makes you happy. You need to be mentally prepared to withstand that rubbish. It provides the sort of happiness that is temporary at best. If those companies persuade you to buy something you can't really afford, just watch – it'll soon make you unhappy instead.

When we're stressed is when we're the most likely to make bad money decisions. It's the perfect time for a company to wave a shiny promise of happiness in front of you, because your brain just wants to say yes – even if your stress is caused by a lack of money.

Finance company Credit Karma released a US-based study at the end of 2017, which found 52 per cent of American consumers would impulse buy to deal with feeling stressed. Of those people who were stress-spending, 60 per cent of them did it on a monthly basis. They spent too much, started to become stressed about it and then, to avoid those bad feelings, they bought something else to make themselves feel better.

This works for about five minutes. Then you don't feel better anymore. Reality comes crashing back in and your stress levels go up even higher.

Many people will fund this cycle with debt, which means that they're paying extra money for simply having something faster. You have to pay the money back eventually, and when you do, you will pay more because of the interest and fees they charge.

If you could have the exact same thing for $50 or $100, why on earth would you pick the $100 option? Why would I hand over money I've worked hard for to a financial company just for the fun of it? That doesn't sound fun at all.

A credit card is not 'your' money, and the card limit is not how much you have available to spend. It's how much the company is willing to lend to you – and charge you for the privilege.

Many of us intuitively understand this, but don't want to admit that we're guilty of it ourselves. The natural response when you get yourself into financial hot water is to close your eyes and pretend it isn't happening. Maybe take the car out for a spin and try not to think about the looming repayment. Or shove that expensive dress to the back of your wardrobe, never to be worn, in case you feel the sting of the credit card bill when you do.

It's a totally natural response to bury your head in the sand, but eventually those credit card companies won't let you do it anymore. They'll track you down.

I don't even like the 'buy now, pay later' companies that have cropped up in recent years. I can't tell you how many times I've had smarmy emails from PR companies, offering up companies they work with, as someone to come onto my podcast and talk about how their credit system will help my listeners manage their money better. How generous of them!

Unfortunately for them, I don't buy their spin.

Those companies that let you spread out your repayments only exist because they're good at getting you to spend money you shouldn't. Shops agree to work with the buy later schemes because it means people spend money they wouldn't otherwise. The purchase is spread out into lots of little payments, so you don't notice it as much.

It feels smaller – but it isn't.

In fact, there's an argument that it's just another marketing gimmick. AUT's Sommer Kapitan has looked into it, and says the likes of After Pay and Lay Buy appeal to a younger generation, which saw the financial crisis and are now scared of credit cards. Meanwhile, the pay later schemes promise no interest and smooth out the payment process, so you can buy what you want.

As Sommer also points out, the companies don't check your ability to actually pay for the items and they'll sting you with fees if you miss a payment. It's easy to lose track of all the little payments and rack up more debt than you intended to.

Predatory lenders are defined by not checking whether a person can afford the debt they're taking on and charging unreasonable fees compared to the size of the loan. When you look at it this way, some of these companies are getting close to the predatory line.

Of course, while I don't like those companies, they're nothing like pay-day lenders. Those guys often charge more than 50 per cent per year or maybe even 1 per cent per day. There's no maybe about that situation: that's predatory.

Remember how beautiful compound interest can make your wealth grow bigger and bigger without you even looking at it? Well, debt also compounds. Except it compounds in a way that hurts you. The longer you take to pay it off, the more you pay overall, with that money snowball rolling along to make your debt bigger over time. You want debt to be paid off as fast as you can because time is literally money.

I'm talking a lot about the worst examples here, but the way to treat debt is always the same. Car loans, credit cards, your mortgage – you avoid them if you can, and if you can't, get them paid off and get them gone quick, ideally faster than the minimum repayment rate demands.

Compound interest can both help and hurt you. It helps with investments, but hurts with debt. Time truly is money.

Whatever interest rate you're being charged, debt is a millstone around your neck. Salvation Army financial mentor Damien Hazlewood says high-interest debt is the biggest struggle for his clients. Clothing trucks, pay-day loans and many other sharks create a vicious cycle for the people he sees.

Those clothing trucks are horrible. They often ratchet prices up by 200 or even 300 per cent. Despite the name, they sell all sorts – electronics, perfume, groceries – and all at hugely inflated prices. They offer loans to people who can't afford those prices, often at extremely high interest rates. They convince people to spend money on overpriced items, which then become more expensive by the second because of the loan.

At the beginning of my career, I lived in a cheap part of South

Auckland, because I needed somewhere with low rent. I had never seen those clothing and groceries trucks before moving to Flat Bush, but suddenly, they were everywhere. They literally patrolled the streets. They were actively targeting a low-income neighbourhood filled with the people who would be unable to pay, but didn't have the financial education to know they were being scammed.

It was a nasty lesson. There are companies out there that exist purely to take advantage of you. If they see blood in the water, that's exactly when they'll target you the hardest.

Damien has had people come to him saddled with debt after a clothing truck followed them down the street, pestering them to buy something. One even waited outside as a woman went to pick her child up from kindy, sending someone in to ask about her while she was inside. Apparently this is a tactic they use – trying to get people to buy something purely to avoid conflict. The worst part is it works.

These people are then stuck with high-interest debt for something they never wanted, which soaks up their limited money. They end up short on cash, so have to go back to the trucks to buy groceries because they need to use the loan system. As their finances become more precarious, the customer leans more and more on the very 'services' dragging them down.

The trucks are an extreme example, but these tactics exist in various forms across lots of different industries. They all want you to spend money and they don't really care how it impacts your life. They just want to get the sale from you.

'You get a loan for $500, and you can easily pay back $1000 even if you follow all the rules,' Damien says. 'Then if you don't make the payments on time, it quickly goes to $1500 or $2000. That's where people end up struggling, and they come to us and say "I've been paying this for years, I just can't get ahead, what do I do?"'

Well, even if you're already in debt, there are tactics to help you. The Commission for Financial Capability's personal finance editor Tom Hartmann says debt is like fire; you have to master it. 'Fire can be useful, but it's also extremely dangerous. We talk about compound interest, but it can compound against you with debt. So what we have there is a fire that starts to rage out of control. Sometimes you can use it to increase your wellbeing, but other times it can take over your life completely.'

What he's talking about there is what some people refer to as 'good' or 'bad' debt, or what I discussed earlier with smart and dumb debt. Some debt can improve your life; you can buy a house, maybe carry out renovations, it can help you build a business. If you're using debt that you can afford to pay off, and that debt will increase your wealth in some sort of way, then there's an argument for it.

'Ideally you would only use debt for things that will increase in value over time,' Tom says. 'Meanwhile something that decreases in value like a car, cars can really destroy wealth.'

Other times people have to use debt to pay their bills or they use debt to fund impulse spending on things that are worth nothing at all. People turn to credit cards when an unexpected expense comes up and they have no savings. None of those things improve your wealth, and they can be the beginning of a debt trap.

The faster you try to get hold of money, usually the more you will pay. Something like a mortgage that takes a lot of planning and is paid off over a long time has a lower interest rate. Meanwhile a credit card, or worse a pay-day lender, will get you money faster, but will charge you a lot more for it.

THE HIGH INTEREST DEBT is some of the most dangerous there is. It can rage out of control because you end up paying so much more than you ever planned, partly because of the way our brains work. We can remember individual purchases we made, but we struggle more to keep the total in mind. Then you get the credit card bill at the end of the month, and you think, wow, did I really do that?

Credit cards particularly are such a convenience, but they are designed to get us to spend more. Some studies even show they have us spend about 30 per cent more than we would if we were using cash.

There are grey areas, because to go back to cars, you might need to get your family around or get yourself to work. Even in grey areas, you need to go in with your eyes wide open. Ask yourself, what is this debt contributing to my life and am I ready to pay the cost?

If you're seeing your wellbeing go down, anxiety going up, you're losing sleep, then it's not worth it and it's time to get rid of it.

Tom Hartmann – CFFC

IT'S AN INTERESTING WAY of looking at a tricky problem. When you look at your wellbeing, and whether a debt will help you get ahead in more than one way, it takes it back to what debt should be. Debt is a tool to be used only when needed. In fact, that's true for money in general.

Of course, you could always twist this and lie to yourself – tell yourself that a debt-fuelled holiday will make you happy and therefore is good for your wellbeing. Memories and new experiences are nice, but you don't have anything to show for it at the end. I love travel, but I don't use debt to fund it. You know when you're kidding yourself. Don't do that.

When you talk to people in the industry, there are plenty of debt horror stories. Sometimes a pay-day lender is used to buy a new TV, a new couch, or, yes, pay for a holiday. If people are struggling to pay their daily expenses because of rock-bottom wages, that's one version of the debt trap. It's a little harder for me to help you fix that; that's a social issue we need to address as a country. But there's also the version where people simply want a bunch of stuff, so put it on the credit card.

It's easy to look at your friends' nice clothes, some Instagram holiday pictures, the home makeover on TV, but that stuff won't make up for the gnawing anxiety of the debt you use to get it. The people you're envying may also be struggling under the weight of debt; you don't know other people's situations. But you know yours. That's all you need to worry about.

I've had people message me to talk about their own debt situation. Some of them describe just a vague feeling of disquiet, but some of them say they feel like they're drowning. Others say it's crushing them. For others, it's in the back of their mind all the time and they're too scared to think about it for long, worrying about what will happen as soon as they slip on this tightrope.

You're not alone. This is really common. We can fix this. We can probably fix it far faster than you realise, but what's important is that we need to fix it quickly.

Whenever I talk to one of these money gurus, the first thing they want people to do is pay off any debt. Make a budget, free up some money and, before you do anything else with that cash, cut the debt.

Authorised financial adviser Tim Fairbrother says people are often overwhelmed by just figuring out where to start with their money. For most of us, the timeline looks like this: set a budget; get out of debt; make sure you have a cash savings account for emergencies; get a KiwiSaver with all of the wonderful free money that comes with it; save for a house; pay off extra on the mortgage; and then start thinking about investments.

For those in the younger generation who've spent years dealing with a housing crisis, hearing 'buy a house' so high up on the list is understandably frustrating. That's where it's useful to remember the timeline is a general structure of the best way for the average person to get ahead. Depending on where you live, maybe the 'buy a house' step needs to be skipped until later, or maybe you'll have to make some big sacrifices to get there. I talk about that in chapter 12.

I would point out that if you want personal financial advice for your particular situation, a financial adviser can help you sort out solutions for the curly problems. Tim works with all types of people, from people who live on a benefit and solo parents on low incomes, to high-flying business people. While some situations are tougher, he reckons he's able to balance anyone's books.

Most financial advisers in New Zealand will give you a free half-hour of their time, so you can run your big problems past them and figure out if you work well together. If you're worried about how to find one, try Financial Advice New Zealand (financialadvice.nz). Only authorised financial advisers can join, and the website lets you search for people in your area, and by topic. Then, it's simply a matter of making sure that you work well together. There's also MoneyTalks (www.moneytalks.co.nz), a free government programme that has money mentors only a phone call or email away. Those are great places to get financial advice, which is specific to your situation, rather than the general rules of thumb I'm talking about here.

Most financial advisers in New Zealand will give you a free half-hour of their time, so you can run your big problems past them and figure out if you work well together.

But back to starting on debt. Yes, it needs to come first.

Sometimes people have told me they have a clever plan where they will invest first, earn money on those investments and then pay off the debt. But any debt that is costing you in interest is a priority over investments. You have to be earning a lot on an investment for it to make more money than debt is costing you.

PAYING OFF DEBT IS definitely the better option, because if you invest money, say you get a return, then you have to pay tax on that. People often forget that part. You might get an average 7 per cent return, but then take off fees and taxes and you're down to 5 per cent. Of course, if you've got riskier investments, then some years you get a return, others you don't.

When you're paying off debt, those interest payments are certain, they're locked in. You're paying that.

Tim Fairbrother – Rival Wealth

WHEN YOU HAVE A debt that you pay off early, it's like making money because you just saved yourself the interest that you would have paid. Is the interest rate 18 per cent? Congratulations, you just made an 18 per cent return.

Of course, it would have been better not to have the debt in the first place because you'll have paid something for it, but that's how life goes. Just pay it off and then avoid debt in the future.

I'm thankful that of all the mistakes I've made, racking up big debts hasn't been one of them. We've talked previously about how I know that I'm a spender. I'm prone to impulsive decisions, which I regret later. My husband is the saver. But at the very least, I've always been honest with myself about this, so I've never trusted myself with a credit card or a car loan. The only good thing about when I had a bad relationship with money was that I feared debt. I avoided almost all types of debt because I knew it would spiral quickly. I no longer fear debt; it's a tool, like anything else to do with money. But I still stay away from it.

Even now, I don't have a credit card but my husband does. It's the equivalent of having a financial sponsor. I only really need credit if I want to buy something online, and I do know the credit card number. I'll use it as a method of payment when I have the money in my account already, then I immediately pay it back. I don't ask permission; I'm a grown woman with my own money and good luck to anyone telling me what to do. But he'll still see it on the bill and the thought of him judging me holds me back from anything truly stupid. It also stops me from being able to lie about my financial situation. Honesty keeps me accountable.It doesn't have to be someone you're in a relationship with. Anyone that you trust with full honesty about your money situation could do some version of this. Use the resources you have.

If you've already fallen into the debt trap, then you need to deal with it. Making minimum repayments can mean that debt sticks around for years and you pay much more overall. There are ways to get that monkey off your back much faster and that will help you pay less overall.

Tom Hartmann has two main strategies for knocking it on the head. You just need to pick the strategy that feels best to you, and keeps you motivated.

Snowball or avalanche to pay off debt faster. Snowball means sniping out the smallest debts, one by one. Avalanche means focusing on the highest-interest debts.

First, there's the avalanche technique. You pick the highest interest debt, then the next highest, then the next. Maybe your car loan is worst. You make the minimum repayments on everything to avoid debt collectors knocking on your door, but all of your extra cash goes into paying down the car loan. Then once it's gone you work on the credit card. You practically ignore the interest-free student loan.

Financially, this makes a lot of sense. By knocking off debts with the highest interest, you'll save yourself the most money in overall interest payments. If you were a robot with no need to worry about emotions, this would be the only way that would make sense.

There is, however, a second way of doing it for those of us who need help with motivation. The snowball technique is where you take out the smallest debt amounts first, no matter what their interest rates are.

This technique keeps human nature in mind. It doesn't matter what technically saves you the most money if you don't stick with it. Snowball helps those of us who need the victory and positive reinforcement of crossing those smaller debts off the list. That's fine. Do whatever you need to do to keep you going.

Whichever one you prefer, you then need to look at how much money you have left after core expenses and dedicate as much of that as you can to paying off the debt. Assassinate those debts one at a time, avalanche or snowball style.

The only right way to pay off debt is the way that works.

Tom does warn that the one thing you shouldn't do is try to pay off all debts at once. It doesn't help your motivation and it doesn't make much financial sense. Pay your minimum requirements and focus all your extra money on one debt at a time.

If you're truly in over your head, at the time of writing the Salvation Army has a no-interest loan scheme (www.salvationarmy.org.nz). You can apply for them to take over your debts and set up a payment plan for you to pay it off, without the interest that makes the loan keep building up bigger and bigger. Theirs is the only one I know of that operates nationwide, but there are also similar local programmes in various cities around New Zealand. There are resources and programmes to help you. Look for them and use them.

Even if you pay off debts, there's a new trap that you need to be careful of: you still need to change the money behaviour that got you into trouble in the first place.

If you don't change your money mindset and cut up those credit cards that got you into hot water in the first place, then you'll likely see that clear balance the same way a bull looks at a red rag. You'll go charging straight for it and start spending beyond your means again.

This is something that happens quite often when people use consolidation loans. Some people choose to consolidate, or combine, their multiple debts into one low-interest loan. So far, so good. That's a decent way to pay off your debt – on paper – but it frees up those cards and lenders that got you into trouble in the first place. And some people see those clear balances and just can't stop themselves spending all over again.

IT'S ABOUT REMEMBERING HOW people work. Consolidating your debt can be a good idea financially. But you need to change your mindset and your behaviour. If you don't change how you use debt, debt consolidation can actually wind you up and allow your debt to rage even more out of control.

If you're going to do debt consolidation make sure you've got rid of all the ways you can continue to borrow, and make sure you've got yourself set up so you can operate within your budget, not just racking up more debt.

Tom Hartmann – CFFC

IF YOU REALLY, TRULY, have to use a loan, then make sure you read the fine print and know exactly what you're getting into. If you know what you're looking for, you can avoid the worst of the worst.

A LOT OF THESE contracts are quite hard to read, but you should ask the provider, what are the fees, so they can point them out on the contract. Then look at the interest, how high it is, actually figure out how much you will pay all up.

Look for interest-free terms, then make sure you pay it off within the interest-free period. A surprising number of places do interest-free now. There are also places that still offer lay-by.

Damien Hazlewood – Salvation Army

OF COURSE, NO DEBT at all is much better; but sometimes life happens and a bit of knowledge can make sure you only shoot yourself in the foot, rather than blasting off an entire limb.

Damien says he's worked with people who went from having debt collectors knocking on their door to eventually saving up to buy a car with no debt. Some even cleared their debt, started a savings habit and were soon able to head off on an overseas holiday. It can be done.

The trick is to avoid telling yourself it's pointless to even try. There are things within your power and people who can help you. You won't get ahead by doing the same things you've done until now. Talk to the people who know more and will use that knowledge to help you.

This is why I get so irritated by things like status symbols. It's no small thing trying to wean yourself off the debt trap. We're bombarded by companies promising the world, if only you'll part with some cash. Many of these companies will even try to convince you that they're just here to help. Among the more annoying sales pitches I've seen was an ad where they offered a loan 'so you can get a ring big enough for her to say yes'.

If you need a ring 'big enough for her to say yes', find yourself a new girlfriend.

Around the time that it became clear my now-husband and I were probably thinking about marriage, I mentioned to my husband that he had better not buy me an expensive ring. For starters, I'm terrible at losing things and didn't need the pressure. Secondly, I intended to pay for half of the engagement ring myself and didn't want to pay thousands.

This might not sound terribly romantic to you and that's okay. To each their own. I can assure you that when he did take me by surprise and propose on a beach, which had special significance to me, my world stopped for a few seconds. Then I burst into tears. It was plenty romantic for me and I wouldn't change a thing.

I've managed not to lose that engagement ring, but I am now onto my third wedding ring. My cat ate the first one (cat lady problems, right?), I plain old lost the second one and so far the third one is hanging in there.

Now, this wouldn't be so bad if I had been as sensible with my wedding ring as I was with my engagement ring. But I did get sucked in momentarily on the lie of 'needing' a flashy wedding ring because I would be wearing it for the rest of my life. The first one was an expensive white gold band, set half way around with small diamonds. It lasted about 18 months before my cat ate it. Sigh.

At least I paid cash for it and wasn't having to keep making repayments on a ring decorating the inside of my cat.

The second and third rings looked exactly the same, but instead of costing me $1000, they cost $30. They're stainless silver and cubic zirconia from that lovely chain store Lovisa. I stumbled across them while looking for cheap earrings. Truly, the design looks identical. If I end up losing my wedding ring yet again, I'll also get the fourth from Lovisa.

I've been sucked in worse in the past though. When I had even less money to pull myself out of a hole.

When I was at university, it was worryingly easy to get credit and get into debt. In my student years, there was a trend of banks posting employees through the common areas on campus, offering you something like a $40 sweetener if you signed up with them. That sounded like a great deal at the time. While you signed up, they made sure to tell you that you could get an interest-free overdraft.

I was at university for six years. I know – far too long. I got an undergraduate degree, an honours degree, a Master's degree, panicked midway through Master's because I realised I wasn't qualified for anything I wanted to do, then got a postgraduate diploma in journalism. This path was unnecessarily long and I don't recommend it.

By the time I was reaching the end of my studies, I had no reserves left, no savings and very little time for a part-time job as I was busy working for free to try to break into my chosen industry. In order to do that free work, I needed work appropriate clothes, but I couldn't afford them. So I racked up a $2000 overdraft in the last six months of my university life, just trying to get by. I almost made it. But that last 8 per cent of my university time was make or break and it came pretty close to break.

It hadn't felt like debt because it was an overdraft rather than a credit card. It was interest-free when I set it up but, as soon as I was employed, my bank account changed from a special student account to just a regular old bank account. The overdraft started costing me in fees, and yet I put off dealing with it for another four years.

Like everything else, I decided to deal with it at the same time I admitted I needed to change my money relationship in general. The weird part was when I admitted I had a problem, I actually took the sting of stress and worry out of it. I was able to break my stress-spend cycle by taking a hard look at my flaws and then refusing to be ruled by them anymore.

I started out by trying to be more 'money aware'. So I was scrolling through my bank transactions one day when I accidentally caught sight of the overdraft fee – $25 a month. The little fee irritated me. Maybe it was small, but it was stupid and unnecessary, and I knew it had been leaving every month for the last four years.

All it took was the decision to do something about it and a pen and paper. I sat down and figured out how much I paid in rent and bills, put aside a small amount for treats (just enough to stay sane) and cut my auto-payments to the savings account as paying off debt was more important. By the time I was done, I was able to set aside $500 a month to pay off my overdraft.

I still wasn't earning much at this point. From memory, I think it was just under the average national wage – but once it was a priority, lo and behold, within four months, it was gone. All it had taken was the decision to actually do it.

It took four months of determination to pay it off, but over the previous four years of ignoring it that $25 per month added up to $1200 – over half of what I'd borrowed in the first place. No wonder the banks think it's worth their while sending staff to target university students.

I was still lucky because my minor dabble with debt hadn't led to missed payments or fees building up. When that happens, you get a bad credit rating and that quickly makes life harder. If you're concerned about it, you can check your credit rating with free online services, so that you at least know where you stand.

ONCE YOU HAVE DEFAULTS or other things on there that make your credit rating drop, at least you can see what's going on. So if there are outstanding debts that a client isn't paying, we'll call the creditor and start the payments, and that immediately has the credit history improving.

Your general defaults will be removed fairly quickly, some within weeks. It's only the more serious things like bankruptcy that will stick around for five years.

One of my clients had his own business, but he hadn't set up a business account, hadn't got in touch with an accountant, hadn't sorted out what taxes he needed to pay and had no mentoring for actually running a business. So I came on board and mentored him, only for two or three weeks, but we got him onto all of that stuff. But if I hadn't stayed on his case, he wouldn't have done it, and a year down the track he would have got into trouble.

Some people have a lot of pride and they struggle to ask for help, but if you don't, it can be really hard on your own. You shouldn't feel

ashamed if you don't know. It's like anything, you won't know if you're not taught.
Damien Hazlewood – Salvation Army

MOST OF WHAT WE'VE talked about so far is fairly simple debt – the kind you want to avoid where possible and pay off quickly once you have it. But there are certain types of debt that are a little different and might need a different strategy for paying off.

These days I own a home, which also comes with a mortgage. As I mentioned, a home is usually put into the 'good debt' category because it gives your life stability, and you can use it as leverage to get investment properties or maybe start a business. But what Tom Hartmann said about minimum repayments is still true here. If you're making minimum payments, you're mostly just paying interest. You're not paying back much of the money you were loaned in the first place. You can be strung along paying extra for years.

Now, mortgages are a funny old thing, as the interest on them is lower than, say, a credit card, but they're also kicking around for 30 years or so. Even if you pay it off faster, you're probably talking 20 years, or maybe 10 if you're really hammering it hard.

You need to factor your mortgage into longer-term life plans, more so than other types of debt. Of course, those life plans should include things like making some investments, to give you greater financial stability and create wealth that doesn't rely on you always having a job. But there's a division here amongst the financial smart guys, on whether your priority should be making extra repayments on the mortgage or whether you can also have investments on the side.

Rival Wealth's Tim Fairbrother says even for a mortgage with a small 5 per cent interest rate, your investments would have to go really well to be a better place for your money. 'If the interest rate is 5 per cent, then you have to earn 7 per cent on your investments first, before tax, for it to be equal. So your mortgage gives you an equivalent 7 per cent return straight off the bat. There aren't many investments around that can match that. And the mortgage has no volatility or uncertainty. All that's happening is your balance is going down.'

A mortgage is a sure thing, a good place to put your money and save yourself in the future. Any investment might earn you a lot some years and nothing others. It's hard to compete with a mortgage when you look at it that way.

Meanwhile Tom Hartmann takes the middle ground. He says that while you would typically avoid investing until you have paid off debt, because a mortgage is such a long-term debt, you could arguably do both. 'A mortgage is a sure-fire return in that you'll pay it off, avoid extra interest and without the risk that comes with investing and looking for returns. So that all makes sense, but there are exceptions.

'To take advantage of the compound interest from investments, you need a decades-long timeframe. A lot of people like to do both, so you pay down the mortgage a bit faster while also investing a bit more. The more you can do in both areas, the better off you'll be.

'It really depends on how you run the individual numbers and

Volatility How much an investment will go up and down. Volatility is not the same as risk or return, but the three can be closely linked.

what money you have. Often you'll see the mortgage works out better at first, but you're cutting yourself off from compounding investment returns at the other end. It's not cut and dry for everyone.'

David Boyle from Mint Asset Management is at the other end of the scale entirely. He was horrified at the idea of only starting to invest once a mortgage was paid off. 'I used to look after mortgages when I worked at a bank. Most mortgages are a table mortgage, which means all of the interest is piled at the beginning; you're not paying much of the money you borrowed for the first few years. Then at the end it slides down to where you're paying the money you borrowed back.

'Maybe that [waiting to invest] would work if you stayed in that house forever, but people get a bigger house, they move, things change. It depends how much you borrow, but you do want to get that mortgage down to a timeframe that you can manage. The faster you pay it off, the less interest you pay. But you don't want to never invest. You'll build up one asset, but what you're missing out on is the ability to diversify how you invest.

'Having all of your money tied up in a house is one thing, but you can't sell a bedroom to go on a retirement holiday. People often talk about downsizing, but when it comes to it, they don't want to move.'

It's not that one of these experts is right and the others are wrong; it's a good demonstration of why different strategies work for different people. You need all of the information, then you need to apply it to your particular life situation.

These thoughts were kicking around in the back of my mind

Diversification Buying more than one thing, i.e. not putting all your eggs in one basket. The idea is that spreading yourself across more things protects you from bad luck in one of them.

when I got a small pay rise. It wasn't much – around $20 more a week. It's the sort of amount that could easily be absorbed into day-to-day living without noticing much difference, but I was in full money-scheming mode by then.

I wanted to do something with this little extra, so, out of interest, I googled mortgage calculators to see what difference $20 a week could make to our mortgage. I plugged in how much we owed, how much we currently repaid, and up it came: the standard 30-year mortgage. I popped in the extra $20 a week. It knocked off just under five years.

An amount that I could easily fritter away without noticing it, could have me living mortgage-free five years earlier. Paying it off faster meant I never had to pay some of the interest at all, meaning that $20 was worth far more than $20. There's that compounding rearing its head again.

It occurred to me that if I wouldn't miss $20 a week, my husband probably wouldn't either. Maybe he would even match it.

I changed the figures in the mortgage calculator so that this time we paid off an extra $40 a week between us. This time, we were down to a 22-year mortgage. For an extra $20 a week each, we could have freedom from our mortgage eight years earlier. To put it another way, it would cut out a quarter of our previous repayment time. Bargain.

I'll tell you more about my investing plans later, but basically, I've decided to try to get the best of both worlds. I put a little extra on the mortgage and a little into other investments like shares. It's not as much as I would do if I concentrated solely on one or the other, but that's okay. We've already seen how powerful $20 a week can be, so by putting a bit onto both my mortgage and investments, I like where I'm at.

I only have so much money, but I like the idea of putting a little extra into multiple things. It's basically diversifying my investments – both a house and some shares. I'm in the compounding years of my life, so I want to lay the foundations now for investment returns later.

If the sharemarket takes a dive, as it does every few years, I can still feel comfortable and secure in my home, knowing that things would have to get seriously, badly, gnarly before the bank would try to take it away from me. If I continue the way I'm going, the bank soon won't be able to take it off me in any situation. It'll just be mine and Ben's.

It seems so obvious, but then most of this personal finance stuff is. People tell you 'oh make extra repayments, it clears the debt faster', but I never realised that such a small payment would clear the debt *so* much faster. The trick is any extra repayment goes straight on to the 'principal' debt, meaning the amount you were loaned in the first place. It's almost like making a double payment where you wipe off a bunch of future interest payments at the same time.

I was scared of debt before I started my personal finance journey, but I'm not any longer. Mostly, it's something to be avoided. I only use it for the things that improve my wellbeing. But I understand how to use it properly in those times when I need it.

This attitude change means I rarely feel stressed about money these days, which helps to keep the good cycle going. There's plenty of evidence that shows you need to get your headspace right to deal with the debt. You might assume you have to get your money sorted in order to feel less stressed; but the evidence points the other way. Get less stressed and you'll have a clear head to evaluate your money.

Some people recommend exercise to reduce stress levels. Others think meditation is better. Cutting out toxic influences always helps. Maybe you have your own stress-buster – as long as it's not retail therapy.

The University of Texas even did a study that said keeping a boring old diary has a noticeable impact on stress levels. When you write down your emotions, it takes the sting out of them. If you're keeping a money diary, then there's a double bonus, because you can also take a clear look at what sets you off on a string of bad spending. Then you know what to keep an eye on in future.

It's funny because I look at all of that advice and have to stop myself cringing. It seems so touchy-feely, the sort of things people recommend as a Band-Aid solution to serious problems. Then I remembered that I was writing this book as I overhauled my own money habits. It's basically my own money diary. And it worked.

8.

If you want to be happy, get a savings account

AN INTERESTING THING ABOUT my personal finance journey is that the more I open up about money, the more other people want to talk to me about theirs. This is awesome because I truly believe one of the best things we can do is share our own experiences and learn from the people around us.

However, it's also revealed a strange phenomenon where people often skip straight from being uninterested in personal finance to wanting to play around buying shares. The boring foundations that everyone needs, like setting up a savings account, setting up KiwiSaver right and paying off debt – they just don't seem to get people as excited.

Unfortunately, just like eating broccoli, you've gotta do that stuff. And just like eating broccoli, you'll find if you approach it right, you'll actually develop a taste for it. Butter and garlic are the secret to broccoli, feeling smug and more secure is the equivalent for money.

That's because the boring stuff that you already know you should be doing is secretly the key to feeling good about your money. I'm not kidding. Setting up and actually paying into a savings account could be the thing that gives you the most payoff in terms of money happiness. This is from the ANZ Financial Wellbeing Survey 2018, which looked at whether we're coping with our money and, most importantly, how we feel about it. The results showed two changes had a disproportionate effect on money happiness: not borrowing for day-to-day expenses, and saving regularly.

SAVING REGULARLY AND NOT borrowing for expenses gives a boost to financial wellbeing whether people earn a little or a lot. Even saving a little bit has a powerful effect on how good people feel about their money situation. Rich or poor, small savings or big, this is really important for your money happiness.

No, investments don't count as your emergency fund or savings account. For one thing, it takes a few days, and probably more like weeks or months, to get money out of whatever investment you favour. For another, you shouldn't suddenly sell an investment because your car broke down. You should sell when the time is right for you and the market is in your favour. Selling suddenly is a recipe for losing money.

The experts agree that for both your financial and mental happiness, you've gotta have that cash savings account.

THE REALLY INTERESTING PART was that you would think there was a correlation between financial wellbeing and income, but the things that had an impact were true whatever income you were on. You can look the same on paper, but how you use your money can totally change your financial wellbeing.

I think it's about control. It's about feeling like you're in control, and if something happens, you have the ability to manage it. You're not going to get into some sort of debt spiral. You can be very wealthy, but spending all your money on large cars and large homes and have a huge amount of debt.

A simple thing that can throw people out is that the car needs repairing. That's the type of thing that's unexpected, and the car is super important to get you to work or get your kids around. If you don't have an emergency fund or savings, you still won't really have a choice about needing to pay that expense.

Antonia Watson – managing director, retail and business banking, ANZ

REMEMBER SALVATION ARMY FINANCIAL mentor Damien Hazlewood, who had the great advice about debt? He says the

The two changes that have the biggest impact on increasing money happiness:

1. **Not borrowing for day-to-day expenses**

2. **Saving some money regularly, even if it's a small amount**

Source: ANZ Financial Wellbeing Survey, 2018

best way to avoid that debt trap in the first place, is to have a savings account. 'Most of my clients fall into debt because they've got nothing saved, nothing for emergencies. If someone passes away in the family, they're then expected to help with funeral costs, but they've got nothing. Or the car needs repairs, so they get a loan to get things done. They've got no savings and that's how things start. You get a loan, and then very quickly you're in a bad cycle.'

Personal finance nerds bicker amongst themselves about how much you should have stashed away in a savings account for emergencies. It's a bit of a Goldilocks problem, where you don't want too little, but you also don't want too much sitting in the savings account.

Like I said, the good thing about cash is that it's easily accessible. An emergency hits, you shift around a few things between bank accounts and you're sorted. No paperwork, no waiting for months for it to clear, just problem solved.

Until that emergency comes up, that money is just sitting in a bank account. It's not doing very much except for earning a very little bit at a low interest rate. It's hard not to see it as a missed opportunity when it could be earning you more if you used it to buy something like shares.

That conflict is why the nerds bicker. Everyone agrees you should base your emergency savings on your daily expenses, to give you a certain amount of time that you could survive if a crisis hits. But some say you should have one month of expenses saved, some say three months. Others even say you should have six months of expenses sitting there. It's a jungle of opinions and there are plenty of monkeys on this topic.

My take? I think the reason nobody can agree is because there isn't actually one 'right' answer. There's just a bunch of factors to take into consideration. It's more important to know what those factors are, so you can weigh them up for yourself.

Where are you now? If you were suddenly fired, how long could you pay the bills for? If you injured yourself and the ACC paperwork took weeks or months to clear, what would you do until it came through? Life happens, all the time. You need cash to get you through the first shockwave while you figure out your next move.

Base your emergency savings on your daily expenses to give you a certain amount of time that you could survive if a crisis hits.

The savings account is the part of financial responsibility that I personally struggle with the most. When I buy shares, I feel like I'm buying something fun. I do it each month when I get paid, and I enjoy picking which fund I'm going for this time. I'm a spender, remember. It feels like spending.

It's also true that, just like the research found, when I'm saving regularly and I have that buffer in place, I genuinely sleep better at night. I've managed to put aside about one month of expenses in my personal savings account. That sounds low, but my husband also has his own emergency savings and we have joint emergency savings as well. All up, between us, it probably fluctuates around three months of expenses saved. Maybe it should be more, but it's worked for us so far.

I don't have kids to worry about, and right now I'm focused on putting the rest of my money into the mortgage, KiwiSaver and wealth-generating shares. As with everything to do with money, you've got to think about your situation and what you think you need.

For ANZ's Antonia Watson, she keeps her own emergency fund at around three months of expenses. 'The interesting thing about the survey is that even $1000 will make you much happier and protect you against the unexpected. But three months of your salary, well, that protects you if you have to take unexpected leave or you lose your job. It buys you more time.'

The idea of saving that much money might sound absolutely impossible to you. For some people, it really will be. But that's not true for the majority of us. For many of us, it's just a case of choosing to make it a priority.

Start by going back to your budget. Look at your unavoidable expenses, leaving out all the stuff you can get by without. I mean physical needs, not things that are important to you, but won't kill you to lose for a while. Figure out how long you want to be able to pay these for in an emergency, how much money that is in total, then work towards it.

When BNZ released their 2017 Financial Futures Research it showed just how important this is. One in five New Zealanders don't have any savings at all. Almost half of us have less than

$1000. While there will be people who are living in very difficult financial situations, it simply isn't true that half of all New Zealanders need to spend everything except $1000 in savings. Many of us could be doing a lot better.

If your car breaks down, if your tooth becomes infected, if your company suddenly folds and you are out of a job, you will need more than $1000. These things happen. I'm not trying to scare you, I'm trying to warn you.

THAT'S ENTIRELY INSUFFICIENT. PARTICULARLY in a country like New Zealand where you have weather events that you can't control or you have earthquakes, heaven forbid. Health events that you haven't planned for. If two bad things happen at once, then what? You'll have to make trade-offs that you don't want to make. That can be solved by having a rainy day account.

I personally have at least three months of expenses saved. I think three months, if not more, is a good measure. I think once you have a budget and you've sorted out how much more you could put aside, people are surprised at how quickly that rainy-day fund builds up. Then it becomes a habit, like getting up and having breakfast every day. Habits form quickly.

Donna Nicolof – BNZ

MARTIN HAWES IS CHAIR of the Sumner KiwiSaver Investment Committee and has written several books on personal finance.

He says the people who get ahead are the ones who make sure that saving is built into their life, so that they barely have to think about it.

'Make it automatic and increase it as you go through life. When you get a pay rise, add that to your savings. You've been living on your previous amount, presumably pretty happily, and if you can put aside the new amount you'll really start to get ahead.

'Most of finance and certainly all of budgeting is less about skills. It's more about your attitude and habits. The skills required for budgeting are simply addition and subtraction.'

That doesn't mean waiting for a pay rise though. It means setting up an automatic payment now, for whatever you can afford, that goes straight from your normal account into your savings the day after you're paid. Then if you get a windfall like a pay rise, make the most of it.

If I say 'I'm going to live like a monk this month and everything at the end is going straight into savings', then guess what, it will probably be $3. If I can find a place that sells cheap coffee on the last day then I'll spend that $3 too.

The only way I actually save is when I do it first, and then make other things fit afterwards. If there's a genuine emergency or a bill to be paid then, sure, that's what the savings account is for. But if you leave the money sitting in your everyday account, then you will find excuses and 'needs' to spend it on. That's human nature, so don't play silly mind games with yourself. Do what works.

9.

You're doing KiwiSaver wrong, and it's costing you

THE FEELING OF SUCCESS that came from small budget changes and wiping out my overdraft gave me the confidence to run a critical eye over everything else I was doing. I was finally hitting goals and successfully putting aside spare money in my savings account. The looming sense of dread had dissipated. I was controlling my own money, instead of it controlling me.

I was also starting to itch for more than just saving a few bucks here and there. I was starting to realise that getting some savings together was only the beginning.

It's unfortunately true that you have to have some savings to draw on in times of need, but the rest of your money should be put to work earning you more money. If you sort that out, it could become an income that keeps you afloat in troubled times, like if you unexpectedly lose your job or have a health problem. How nice would it be to not be a wage slave anymore? That if you had a bad boss or a job you didn't love, you could actually have the freedom to walk away and find something better?

I started to investigate investments. Of course, there's property investment, but it's very difficult to get the deposit together if you're part of the younger generation. And it's not exactly open to that 'a little bit, often' strategy that works best for those of us who are new to this.

I cautiously started to look into shares, only to find – to my surprise – that many of the experts sang the praises of starting with KiwiSaver.

In hindsight, it's blindingly obvious. Even when you're a newbie, you're actually already an investor, and you should start with what you already have. Boring old KiwiSaver is a wonderful, gentle introduction to the world of investing and the sharemarket.

Most working New Zealanders have an account, whether or not they're paying anything into it. That money is then invested for you. It all depends on what type of fund you have, but it's usually some mix of cash, bonds and shares.

Maybe you're one of the few workplaces left with its own retirement scheme, or you work in another part of the world – there's almost always an equivalent retirement scheme floating around, and they're usually candy-coated with free money to persuade you to take part.

Figuring out the system you've got and then working it to your advantage is a smart place to start investing. If I walk down the street and see $20 on the footpath, I don't leave it there. I pick it up.

Don't flick the page just yet. I know many people are scared of shares or think that they're incredibly risky and, worst of all, complicated. Heck, I thought that in the past. Before overhauling my relationship with money, I always felt like 'investing' was something done by old men in suits. At the very least, it was done by people earning six figures.

I soon came to understand that that wasn't right. Wealthy people invest, sure, but they don't invest because they're wealthy. They tend to be wealthy because they invest. The chicken comes before this egg.

But I was far from alone in my assumptions. In July 2018, the Financial Markets Authority released its annual survey on how New Zealanders felt about the financial markets. Older men with high incomes felt the most confident about investing into the financial markets. Women and younger people on low incomes were the least confident. It's one of those issues that becomes a self-fulfilling prophecy pretty quickly.

Many people will say they don't have enough money to start investing; but that's the wrong way to look at it.

EVEN IF YOU START with a very small balance, maybe contributing a small amount, but you do it regularly, that compounding effect will leave people very surprised at the lump sum they can finish with.

Investing isn't just for the wealthy people who already have large sums of money. It really is for every age and stage. For young people, even if they only have a small amount, it really is to their benefit to start investing, and investing early.

Mark Fowler – head of investments, Hobson Wealth Partners

IF YOU INVEST A little bit frequently, the idea is that it builds up and makes you less dependent on the job you go to every day. Even better than a savings account, you get side income trickling in, which builds up to a healthier flow every time you contribute to it.

Now okay, for retirement funds like KiwiSaver you can't touch that extra money until you retire, but you do build up a nest egg for the future and learn how investing works. Soon enough, you'll be ready to step up and take on investments outside of the KiwiSaver safety bubble where you can use the income now if you need to. One step at a time, and the first important step is your retirement fund.

This is something I could have learned quite early in my journalism career if I'd just been paying attention. One of my colleagues back then was a very nice man, but was clearly doing the bare minimum and hoping to get a redundancy payout soon. I remarked on it one day to a friend, wondering what the business journalist planned to do if the redundancy worked out and how he would survive without a salary. Their response honestly surprised me.

'But he's a business journalist,' my friend answered, looking at me like I was an idiot. 'He has a cushion.'

'What?' I answered. 'But he's paid the same rubbish as the rest of us, right?'

'Pretty much, but he gets to watch the market and talk to experts all day. Every time he has some spare cash, he invests it.' My friend took in my surprised face, and rolled her eyes. 'Frances, every business journalist is rich. Didn't you know that?'

No. No, I did not know that.

As I have pivoted to do more business journalism, I have unfortunately learned that no, not every business journalist is 'rich'. But they definitely tend to have a better money situation than other journalists, despite being paid similarly. It helps to have the basics of financial knowledge, then you can learn how to protect yourself when a chilly financial wind blows.

Luckily, that's not something that's only open to business journalists. Taking in some expert knowledge is certainly a good idea, but you don't have to talk to them every day. I would actually warn against watching the market every day. Really, you just need to set some investments up then leave them to do their thing. That beautiful compounding.

Each investment you make buys you a piece of independence from bad jobs, bad relationships, hell, a bad life if you're really miserable. One stone at a time, you can build a wall to keep out life's nasty surprises.

That 2018 FMA study found that almost 80 per cent of

18–29-year-olds had a KiwiSaver. Yet they were the group that felt the least knowledgeable and confident about the sharemarket. They almost certainly already owned shares through their KiwiSaver, but that knowledge would probably worry them.

The very first step is to actually put something into your retirement fund. Shocking, I know – but that's actually the biggest problem with KiwiSaver right now. The people who need it most, aren't contributing at all.

In September 2017, ANZ released a white paper reviewing how things had gone in the first 10 years of KiwiSaver. Some of the findings were alarming.

Of those lucky guys earning more than $100,000 a year, 80 per cent use KiwiSaver. That means they get the sweet 3 per cent employer match and the nice government tax break of $521 a year. The perks are as close as you get to a free lunch, and the top earners are making good use of it.

Unfortunately, for people earning less than $50,000 a year, ANZ found only 53 per cent of them are using KiwiSaver. The lower earners were also less likely to have independent savings than the high earners. Where my heart breaks for them the most is that they're missing out on the free employer and government money that they're entitled to, the cash that could make the difference in actually being able to enjoy retirement, rather than slaving away at low-paying jobs until they drop.

When I talked to ANZ's managing director of wealth and private bank Craig Mulholland, he agreed it was concerning. ANZ is one of the biggest KiwiSaver providers.

'There's a group of people, those on minimum wage, where

3 per cent of what they earn is a lot of money to them. But a little bit can turn into a lot, and it's important we help people to save whatever it is that they can afford.'

I mean it when I say KiwiSaver is as close as you get to a free lunch. You don't get many of those in investing, so look after a unicorn when you find it.

You're not just investing your own money and then earning a return on it. Your employer will match you, dollar for dollar, up to 3 per cent of your income. That's free money. Then there's the tax break, where if you put in at least $1042 per year you get $521 from the government. That's a 50 per cent return before you even get started. In fact, depending on your salary, by the time you add up your employer match and the government money, you're doubling your money straight away. And *then* you also get investment returns. Insane. This is a sugar-coated retirement savings plan. All you have to do is contribute to it.

I'm not judging anyone who's struggling to make ends meet and feels like KiwiSaver is in the 'nice to have' category. Maybe you genuinely can't do 3 per cent of your wages to get the full 3 per cent employer match. But even if you can spare just $20 a week to put into KiwiSaver that adds up to $1040 over the year, and just $2 more tips you over the edge to get the entire government tax break. That's an extra $521 a year before you even get any other returns. It will keep earning and compounding for you from then on. You'll still be getting part of the employer match and putting away some money for retirement or a first home.

Craig says that even a little bit would be better than nothing. When he crunched the numbers, he found that if you just put in $1042 a year from the age of 25, by the time you retired at age 65 you would have $250,000. Quarter of a million dollars. That's made up of your contributions, the free money from the government and returns on your investments.

When ANZ researched why people stopped paying into their KiwiSaver, for most, it wasn't actually grinding poverty that was the problem. They found that 80 per cent of people who stopped their KiwiSaver contributions didn't start again for five years. That was the full amount of time allowed in the first 10 years of the scheme. Thirty per cent of the people who did that freely admitted they simply forgot to start payments again.

For the average person who stopped paying into KiwiSaver for those five years, they would then be short $37,000 by the time they retired. Remember, they missed out on the beautiful compound interest on that money.

You need to put money into your KiwiSaver or retirement fund. Today. Even if it's a small amount, even if it feels like it's not enough. Anything is better than nothing.

The second biggest problem, after those who aren't contributing at all, is those damn default KiwiSaver funds.

The average person probably does what I did when I signed up as a 19-year-old – they get handed a form at work, fill it out and then proceed to ignore it. That means you get dumped into a default scheme and sit there. The last time I checked the statistics from the Inland Revenue Department in late 2018, it showed just over half a million New Zealanders sitting in a default scheme.

Just $20 a week will get you the full government KiwiSaver contribution, and some employer money. For most people, that'll double your money.

If you signed up to KiwiSaver, never picked an account and left it at that, you're in a default account. The problem is that these default schemes were never supposed to be permanent. They are a holding pen, which the government set up so that you had a conservative, safe account to start with while you decided what you actually wanted to do with your retirement savings. There's not much risk to them, but there's also very little reward.

There's half a million Kiwis with their money in there, diligently saving into it with each pay cheque and missing out on the rewards for all of their hard work.

The different types of KiwiSaver funds

CONSERVATIVE

BALANCED

GROWTH

AGGRESSIVE

AS A RULE OF thumb, you can put KiwiSaver funds on a sliding scale; conservative, balanced, growth, and aggressive. At the cautious end, you have conservative. Very safe investments, like cash, that are unlikely to go down in value, but don't earn you much, either. At the other end is aggressive, where you might go all in on high-growth shares. You'll make far more money in the long run, but you'll be all over the place in the meantime.

There's nothing wrong with a conservative account if you're, say, saving for a house or about to hit retirement – but you can get conservative accounts that aren't default accounts. There are plenty of conservative accounts with lower fees and better returns than those default funds.

Your KiwiSaver is a huge investment into your future, with many people building up hundreds of thousands of dollars in there. Why on earth wouldn't you spend 10 minutes figuring out your options, when it could mean a difference of hundreds of thousands of dollars in your hand?

Well, except, that was exactly me.

That familiar guilty itch had been scratching away in the back of my mind for a couple of years, telling me that something needed to be done about my KiwiSaver. My retirement savings were, indeed, dumped into a default scheme with one of the major banks. I couldn't even plead ignorance on the issue. I'd read a couple of years before that, that as a person in my twenties, I should have had the money in a higher growth account. With over 30 years until retirement, I had time on my side, so could reap the rewards of higher risk investments and take a few losses in my stride.

Making changes meant taking the time to do it, and somehow

Conservative versus growth investing Conservative investing reduces the possibility of losing the initial investment by investing in less risky assets. Growth investing maximises profits by investing in riskier assets that might go up and down in the short term, but earn more over time.

it was never really a priority. I comforted myself with the knowledge that I was doing more than the minimum. The least you needed to contribute at that time was 2 per cent of your wages, while I had ticked the box for 4 per cent. Four whole per cent! Problem solved. Never mind that the standard rule is to save at least 10 per cent of your salary, if you want a comfortable retirement. Shh! I'm doing more than the minimum. Now praise me.

What I hadn't realised was just how badly I was messing it up by continually not bothering to make the change to a higher growth account, something that would cost me nothing, and would mean hundreds of thousands of dollars more when I retired. Literally.

Picking the type of KiwiSaver fund you want is one of the biggest decisions you can make for your retirement.

YOU NEED TO THINK about this decision early on, and don't postpone this. The whole idea of KiwiSaver is that it's a long-term investment, therefore to make the decision work you have to make it early on.

Choosing the right fund type is the most important choice in front of you, and will have the biggest impact on the wealth that you accumulate over your lifetime. After fund type, it's fees, definitely. But the fund type is the most important, even more than contributions.

Aaron Gilbert – AUT

AGAIN, IT'S DOWN TO compound interest. If you are young and suited for a growth fund, you'll be earning more in returns each year. These stack on top to earn you even more the next year. Your money snowball is moving at speed.

If you're in a conservative fund when you shouldn't be, you're puttering along in first gear. You won't stall, sure, but the engine will be straining and whining while you crawl along – or you can move into fifth gear and cruise along to your destination much faster.

There was another factor paralysing me, though. I was scared of making the wrong choice, of not doing due diligence and getting ripped off. I also wasn't sure how long it would take and who has much spare time these days? Without ever trying, I stuck with the choice that I knew was wrong. How rational.

About seven years into my working life (so much wasted time!) I received an email from the bank, updating me on the growth of my default KiwiSaver scheme. It wasn't much, as I should have expected, because it was a default conservative scheme.

In a fit of inspiration, I emailed them back asking them if I could change to a higher growth scheme. They answered yes, of course I could, but as email was rather insecure, and we were talking about my retirement fund, I'd need to come into a branch to talk to someone.

Ugh. That sounded like a bit more effort than writing an email and having the issue magically solve itself. I put it off for another couple of months.

But it was top of mind now, so eventually I steeled myself and decided to start with the simplest of internet searches – 'KiwiSaver scheme comparison'. Maybe one of my colleagues in the business news department would already have done the hard work for me and written about it in an article.

To my surprise, something even better popped up. An interactive quiz from Sorted (fundfinder.sorted.org.nz or smartinvestor.sorted.org.nz), the website run by the Commission for Financial Capability. I'd struck gold on my first try.

I clicked through and answered a couple of questions about how soon I would need the money, and whether a few ups and downs worried me. As I'd expected, they recommended a growth account. They then asked me if I wanted to compare KiwiSaver growth accounts by the return, the services offered, or the fees charged. Just like that, my top choices were displayed.

The Sorted website also gave a breakdown of where the money was invested, which all looked to be in industries that I was comfortable with. No cluster bomb investments for me, personally. I'm okay with most industries, but a girl has to draw the line somewhere.

I knew I wanted a fund that hit the sweet spot between the lowest fees and the highest returns. I found a good one, put the fund provider into Google, and reassuringly found only awards and praise in the news. That was enough for me.

This time, I was allowed to sign up online. I just needed my IRD number and a picture of my ID. It's amazing how helpful a business can be when they're poaching you from another provider. Just like that, I was in the growth account I knew I needed to be in.

Seven years. Seven years of being in the wrong fund. For three of them I'd known that I needed to change, but I delayed because I was worried I would make the wrong choice, worried I wouldn't know where to start, worried it would be too hard.

In the end, I simply made a decision to look, took about 15 minutes on my laptop and a couple of days mulling it over to be sure. Not exactly difficult.

What I hadn't done yet was work out how much money I'd been throwing away so far. I was about to get a reality check, which would make me relieved that I had made the switch, but mad I hadn't done it sooner.

After my easy experience with Sorted's Fund Finder, I decided to call the people behind it. Hey, it had been really useful for me, so I might as well turn it into a podcast. The Commission for Financial Capability offered up Tom Hartmann, who knew the scheme inside out.

To hammer home how big of a mistake I'd made, he crunched the numbers using me as a guinea pig. He took my salary at the time (I'm not putting that into a book I'm afraid, but I promise we crunched the numbers with my real salary), my age (28 at the time) and assumed I would retire at 65.

If I made the minimum payments into a conservative fund, a reasonable best case scenario was that I could have $285,000 when I retired. If I took the exact same money and paid it into a growth fund, that leapt up by $200,000. I could reasonably expect to have a cushion of $485,000 when I retired.

Those are no small potatoes – for the sake of a few clicks at a computer.

Now, you might also be a little worried about making the wrong choice. The way that I chose my fund worked for me, but might not work for you. Luckily, weighing up the various options doesn't have to be too hard.

First of all, the last time I checked, there were 222 KiwiSaver funds. That's quite a few to check out on your own, so use Sorted to help you figure out your top five. It's independent and uses solid data.

You might be tempted to go for a familiar brand, like the bank you use, but there are far more important things you should think about. The fees they charge, the services and information they offer and their track record of returns will be much more important to your wallet. Sorted has pulled all of that information together for you and will let you rank the funds by the best performers on that criteria.

All you have to do is look at it. That's all your end of the bargain is.

Now, yes, a growth account means that you're taking on 'higher risk', which tends to send people running for the hills. 'Risk', in our general life, means something is not a good idea. Avoid.

That's not necessarily true for investing or thinking about retirement. Risk does mean that, yes, you're taking a risk. It also means that, if you have enough time up your sleeve, on average you'll make more money back. You just have to approach it with a long timeframe in mind, say more than five years, and not put all your eggs in one basket.

The problem is many people in KiwiSaver have never invested, so they tend to think of their KiwiSaver account as a savings account that they can watch going up over time. Heck, some banks will even let you put your KiwiSaver balance right next to all of your other bank accounts, so that you can watch your balance climb a smidge higher every day.

Except that your KiwiSaver account isn't like a savings account. It's a type of investment fund, which means your money is working harder, trying to make you even more money. Some of it might be in shares, some of it in property, some of it in bonds, all depending on what type of KiwiSaver you signed up to.

That's all good stuff for your future, but it means your KiwiSaver can go down too. It's not a bad thing, you just need to be mentally prepared.

AUT finance lecturer Dr Ayesha Scott says a KiwiSaver balance will always go up and down because that's the normal market cycle. As long as you pick the right fund at the start, you simply wait it out.

You might be noticing a theme here, and, yes, what these experts keep coming back to is that time is one of the biggest considerations for your investment strategy. How soon do you need the money? How long can you bring yourself to leave it? The longer, the better.

I'm young or, at least, in financial terms I'm young. I'm in my early thirties and have bought a house, so can happily whack my money into a growth KiwiSaver account and let it do its thing for another 30 years. I don't need it. Whereas, different life stages might mean other people need a different approach. Time is everything when it comes to thinking about how you want to invest.

IF I WAS AFTER my money within the next five years, I'm getting close to retirement or I want to buy my first house and that's what I'm

Bonds One of the lower risk type of investments, where your money is unlikely to go down, but you also only make a smaller return.

using my KiwiSaver account to do, then I would like to be in a more conservative fund, because five years is perhaps not enough time to ride out a market correction.

More than 10 years is the long term. You have someone like me who is in my early thirties, for me KiwiSaver is a long-term game. I will be saving for my retirement for at least the next 30 to 35 years. I will probably see at least three, maybe four market cycles and corrections while I'm saving for my retirement. For me, it doesn't actually matter, I don't mind if the market corrects a little bit, even a lot, because I'm actually going to get more value for money with my contributions.

As long as I keep putting my money away, this will actually mean I get more for my money over the long term. When the market goes down, I actually feel like I'm investing my money wisely because I'll benefit more from the upswing. If you're still buying when the market is down, the value will increase more later.

Of course, if I was in my fifties, it'd be different. Because then I don't have as much time to wait for the market to go up again after a downturn. Or if you're using KiwiSaver to save for your first home, again, your time horizon is shorter.

This is the old risk and return relationship, which I teach my first-year finance students. Of course, you want to get returns, but you need to take a little bit of risk to do that.

Dr Ayesha Scott – finance lecturer, AUT

IF YOU HAVE TIME up your sleeve like Ayesha and I do, the market highs and lows are simply noise that can distract you. It can be easy to look at a dip, see that what you have is worth less now

Correction A nice little word experts use for when the market goes down. 'The market is going through a correction' sounds less scary than 'Arrrgghhh! Where has all of my money gone?'

and be worried, but both the highs and the lows are a very good thing for your investing future. I mean it – you need the lows.

What Ayesha is saying is that the highs are when you make the money, which is all very nice. But the lows are when you buy investments cheaply, so that you can make that money later. You can't have one without the other. That's the whole point.

Don't panic when things go down. It's great for future you. You're just going sale shopping, as long as you have the time to wait for things to bounce back.

Of course, even in your fifties, you might not plan to use your investing money for another 20 years. So you need to know that time is the biggest factor, and that it's *your* personal timeline that you should be thinking about. You need discipline, but you also need to be honest with yourself.

Ayesha says this is where people get confused about the sharemarket being more volatile. Sure, it's up and down in the short term, but over the longer term, the line between those points steadily goes upwards. You need to think about what's right for you, and then get the most money for your situation.

She says if you go for the longer-term options, you need to remember not to panic if things start to go down. If you yank everything out when the market goes down, you've just turned this into a short-term strategy. It needs to sit there long term, if that's what you've picked to do.

THE WORST THING YOU can do, if the market dips, is to sell. You're selling off your assets cheaply. Sharemarket fluctuations don't actually mean anything unless you're buying or selling. If you're just holding on to those assets, those ups and downs don't matter. It's not until you sell out of an asset that you actually crystallise, or realise, any loss or gain. So your KiwiSaver balance might go up and down, but that is something that just exists on paper.

You need to engage with your KiwiSaver, but please realise that engaging in the process is choosing the correct fund type and how much you put into it. It is not switching and changing the risk levels with market cycles, because that is a sure-fire way to lose out on returns and crystallise losses. You only need to look at it every few years, unless there are some major changes in your own life.

Dr Ayesha Scott – AUT

NOBODY LIKES TO FEEL like they're losing money, but you're not. Once I understood that was how it worked, I was ready to grit my teeth and look away when things got grisly out there.

Now, you could decide that this means shares are not for you. The very thought of all this might make you nauseous, and we always have to keep the human factor in mind. You might even decide you want to change your KiwiSaver scheme, so that it can't be affected by the sharemarket. That's totally your choice, and maybe something like a term deposit is better for you. It's not going to have the same volatility, but you're also not going to get the same return on your money. Personally, I'll grit my teeth and take the cash, thanks.

Jose George, general manager at Canstar, an independent financial research group, is another person who spends time

Term deposit Money you give to the bank to hold for a certain length of time, generally with a better interest rate than a normal savings account.

researching the market, and looking for trends to help you and me out. He put it well when he told me that risk was 'absolutely not' something to be scared of, but just another term to understand.

IF YOU TAKE MORE risks in life, there are potential chances that you could fail, but there are bigger opportunities for you to gain as well. But if we're talking specifically about KiwiSaver, then that's different. The probability of losing your money completely is really, really low, because there are strict rules that mean you're in a well-managed, structured investment. Even a bank deposit is not without risk. But it's really at the lowest end of the risk spectrum, so also, at the lowest end of returns.

Jose George – general manager, Canstar

YOU NEED TO FIGURE out what level of risk you're okay with, and what level of return you want for your future. Then the next thing to keep an eye on is fees.

AUT finance professor Bart Frijns has crunched the numbers on fees. The result is a scary warning about KiwiSaver fees in particular, although if you're looking at investing in any type of managed fund or index fund, the same advice is true.

You get charged a fee any time you invest in shares. Fees can be big or small, but you always need some type of middle man to get you into shares and they charge you a bit for the privilege.

Managed or mutual fund An investment fund run by a person, so usually charges more than an index fund because a real person (and labour) is involved and making the decisions.
Index fund An automated type of investment fund, which automatically tracks and invests in a certain area. The aim is to give a broader market exposure (diversification) for a low cost.

I talk about the how and why of that in more detail in the next chapter, but for now, you just need to understand how they impact your KiwiSaver. If you don't, it could be like letting a golden retriever take a lick of an ice cream. It's never just a lick – they'll take most of it for themselves.

Bart worked out that, for the average person, a fee of just 1.5 per cent over a 40-year period would suck away 20 per cent of the profits you would have earned otherwise. That's the power of compounding in action; you not only pay that money from your retirement fund, you lose everything that money would have earned you over time. Suddenly, that fee is looking a lot more meaningful, right?

He says people often assume that you get what you pay for, yet research shows high fees don't lead to high returns. Even worse, his research showed there was almost no relationship between the fees you paid, and the performance you got. Your odds are just as good with the cheap accounts.

He published some of this research in 2014, with his colleague Alireza Tourani-Rad. They found that KiwiSaver fees were far higher than international standards, and there was no extra performancc to show for it. So it's worth making sure you check what you're paying. Nobody likes being ripped off.

AUT Associate Professor of Finance Aaron Gilbert says there's a wide range of fees charged in New Zealand, from 0.3 per cent up to almost 2 per cent. Those bigger fees can be a retirement killer. 'The real kicker isn't the fact they've taken the fee out, it's that the money then isn't earning anything in the next period. A big part of the fees issue is actually the lost opportunity for compounding.'

Again, the 'get what you pay for' myth comes up. When I asked Aaron about it, he let out an exasperated laugh. 'People assume that if you pay more you get better service. And if you have complicated decisions to make, and you don't really understand what you're doing, it's an easy psychological shortcut. Because quality costs, right? No.

'Some of the worst performing funds over the last ten years have been the most expensive. Whereas the passive funds, they might not be number one in the league tables, not at first. But when they're consistently in the middle of the pack, and saving you big time in fees, then you're way ahead in terms of what you get in the hand.'

To recap: you can have conservative, balanced, growth or aggressive KiwiSaver funds, but any of those can also be active or passive. Conservative, etc. describe the *type* of things you invest in. Passive/active is talking about the *strategy* you take while investing in them. For instance, I am young, but also lazy, and I only pay for something if it's definitely bringing me results. As such, I like an aggressive investing strategy with lots of shares, but in a passive fund where I'm not paying a person to make lots of extra decisions that cost me money without bringing extra results.

Our Canstar friend, Jose George, agrees with the fees warning. He even went a step further, pointing out that the return you get can vary on any given year depending on what's happening in the market at that point. Yet the fees are one of the few things that are totally concrete and certain when you pick a KiwiSaver provider. There's an argument for looking at fees first, and returns second.

Active versus passive investing Active investing is buying and selling regularly, constantly monitoring the area you invest in. Passive investing is trying to pick a good long-term investment then leave it alone to do its thing.

'These days, at Canstar we judge it based on "performance net of fees", so how much is your return once the fees are taken out. That's really important, because at the end of the day it's pointless having a headline return number, if the fees eat most of the return.'

Compounding. It makes your investment returns stronger, it makes the impact of debt worse and it also makes the impact of fees worse.

You can't control everything when you're investing. In fact, most of my investing strategies are built on exactly that – I can't control the market, can't control other investors, so I won't even try.

You *can* control fees. Fees are one of the few fixed costs in investing. Returns aren't guaranteed, but fees are. Get those fees down, so that any profits come to you, not someone else. Then the money you've kept through saved fees will keep on compounding and earning you more. Over 20 years, you're going to be very happy that fee money kept working for you instead of someone else.

If that's all getting a bit overwhelming, then just remember the bottom line. The single biggest difference for your KiwiSaver future is in actively picking a conservative, growth or aggressive fund. It outweighs just about everything else. And it costs you nothing.

For all of the talk about embracing risk for a bigger return, there are still situations where a conservative account will be best. If you've looked into it and decided that's what works for you, that's great. It really might be best for you, whether that's because you want to buy a house soon, you're retiring soon or you simply don't have the appetite for risk that comes with a higher return.

But half a million New Zealanders sticking with the default accounts suggests that they haven't thought about it at all, or they don't realise that they're throwing so much money away. All for the sake of a few clicks at their computer.

It pains me to think of people who are simply unaware of the issue, or who hear 'risk' and shut down without understanding what it means for investments. Imagine carefully stashing your money away with each pay day, thinking that you're doing the right thing. Then it barely grows and when retirement comes, you still have to scrimp and save. When you could have saved the exact same money, put it into a growth account and had a cushy retirement.

If the idea of struggling through your twilight years scares you, then good. Don't think you can just rely on the pension and you'll be fine.

For starters, who knows what future governments will do to the pension? There's mounting pressure for the retirement age to be increased, or for the amount to be cut back. It's basically a matter of time before one government or another gives in to that.

But even if nothing changes, just the pension isn't enough right now. In New Zealand, if you're single, you get around $20,000 a year. If you're a couple, you get around $30,000 a year between both of you.

The situation gets especially bad if you haven't been able to buy a house and pay off the mortgage before retirement. Given the current housing situation, I wouldn't blame you if that was the case. But it would mean you could blow your entire pension just keeping a rented roof over your head. If you haven't taken care of KiwiSaver, what will you eat?

Some of this can seem daunting at first glance, but once you've figured out a couple of rules of thumb, it's honestly not. I took the first step, even though I felt out of my depth, and then the one after that. It wasn't hard, as it turns out. After all, how do you eat an elephant? One bite at a time.

I knowingly held myself back from three years of stronger returns just because I felt unqualified to even look at it. Don't do that.

10.

You are not the exception, you are the rule

ONCE YOUR KIWISAVER OR retirement fund is sorted, that's the time to start thinking about investments to make under your own steam. After all, it's nice to have money working hard for you that isn't locked away until you're 65. Early retirement, a mini retirement break, a career change, life change – having your own investments gives you options.

So back to that interesting switch people make when you talk to them about investing. One minute the stock market is scary and not to be touched, the next they want to jump straight into picking individual stocks or buying into a flashy managed fund that charges like a wounded bull.

This isn't the best idea, but the thinking behind it actually makes sense. We're told that if you work hard and do your homework, you'll get ahead. So, work hard, do your homework on a certain company or fund, then sit back and reap the rewards. Right?

Probably not.

Now bear with me here, because we need to get a little nerdy. I'm going to run you through certain types of investments, so that you know what I'm talking about when it comes to the sharemarket. It won't take long, but you need to pay attention for a bit so that you know what I'm talking about later.

Most people have come across term deposits or bonds before. That tends to be what people think of when you say 'put your money to work'. A term deposit is usually with a bank. You agree not to touch that money for a certain length of time, usually months, and they will pay you interest.

Meanwhile bonds are usually between you and a government, and technically, you are loaning them money. They often pay you back at a fixed rate, which is interest. You'll sometimes hear them referred to as a 'fixed income investment' because you know how much you're getting and when.

Both of these are very safe investments, but the price of that safety is that you're actually not getting much money back as a return. The amount you get changes a bit, because it depends on interest rates. At the moment, interest rates are low, which makes the people with a mortgage happy because their loan is cheaper. It also means term deposits and bonds don't earn much for the savers.

Right now, it's nowhere near enough for me. I might change my mind in the future, because interest rates will inevitably go up, and these investments will make more money. But that process takes years, decades even. I'm young, and have decades until retirement makes me 'need' the money, so it's the perfect time for me to go into long-term investments.

This means I like the sharemarket. There are lots of options for getting into the sharemarket. You can decide to pick which individual companies you like and think will succeed. Or you have funds, where you contribute your money into a pool of money with other investors, and it's then spread around a bunch of different companies. Diversity baby, it's the name of the game and a fund gets you there.

The next thing you need to know is what type of fund you're getting into. The main ones you'll hear about are passive index funds and actively managed funds.

The name of managed funds changes a little depending on what country you're in; look out for managed fund, mutual fund or actively managed fund. All of these mean you have a qualified person who is deciding where your money goes and which investments they think are best. They do some research and analysis of the market, so you're going to be paying a higher fee. That's what you get for the personal touch of a qualified person. Even qualified people don't have the best track record on picking winners though, but we'll talk about that in just a tick.

Now, an index fund has no human touch. Keep an eye out for names like passive investing, index fund or ETF. These technically mean slightly different things, but in practice it usually means an index fund. It invests on a set of rules with everything happening automatically. The index fund will stick to that rule, buying you a little sliver of several companies at once. Because there are no people doing research or making educated guesses, they are much cheaper.

You'll hear people throw around a lot of acronyms when they're talking about the sharemarket, which can make it sound complicated when it's really not. The NZX is our sharemarket – as in New Zealand eXchange. Australian companies have the ASX. In fact, most developed countries have their own sharemarket. You can buy into all sorts of different ones depending on what share account you set up, but we'll get into that later in the chapter.

Then they break out the acronyms again for the different fund types. For example, the Smartshares dividend fund (DIV) will buy shares in the 25 highest-dividend paying companies in New Zealand, or the NZX50, which is the top 50 companies in the New Zealand market. If a new player storms the gates and becomes one of the top 50 companies, the index fund will automatically shift your money into them. You might see a bunch of acronyms on the board at first, but if you just click into them, they'll tell you what they're investing in. They have to. It's a legal requirement.

Any fund will charge you a fee because they're making investments for you, and even automatic computer investing has a small cost. This fee is calculated as a percentage of all of the money you give them. If you have $100 invested and it's an index fund charging 0.5 per cent, they will charge you 50 cents. If it's an actively managed fund charging 1.5 per cent, they'll charge you $1.50. This has nothing to do with how much they earn you that year. It's simply calculated on how much money you put in with them. Fees matter a lot, considering an average investment might earn around 5 per cent in a year. Suddenly, you can be losing a huge chunk of your profits, so pay attention to fees.

I'm nearly done with this bit, but first a small clarification. I mentioned ETF before, with the index funds. Now technically, an ETF is an exchange traded fund, and it can be either actively managed or a passive index fund. The difference with these guys is simply that they're listed on the stock exchange. However, when your average person talks about an ETF, they often mean an index fund, so just double-check that you're on the same page.

Fees matter a lot, considering an average investment might earn around 5 per cent in a year.

There's a similar issue with managed funds. Most of the time when people talk about managed funds, they are meaning an actively managed fund. But there are fund managers who believe in passive management. They just use a human touch to set the rules of the fund, then leave it to passively do its thing.

A lot of ethical funds do this, as ethical investors will be pickier about investments.

These minor clarifications are just so that you know the difference between what a word technically means and how most people actually use it. It's like how the word literally no longer means literally, because too many people say they would 'literally die' to simply express shock.

Right, that's the nerdy stuff done. Back into the fun stuff of how you get that to make you money.

The funds I mentioned are really important, especially when you're first starting out as an investor. That's because, no matter what you're into, you need 'diversification'. That just means don't put all your eggs in one basket. It's essential.

According to Mark Lister, you need to make sure you're spread across several different companies. That doesn't mean just one, or two, or five. He's talking at least 10 or 15. Hopefully even more.

DIVERSIFICATION IS CRUCIAL. It's about reducing your risk, and every study shows that increasing your diversification reduces that potential risk.

You want to have a good exposure to different industries, not just the technology sector, because what if something goes wrong? We want some materials companies, some consumer companies, some banks.

You don't even want all your shares to be in the same region. New Zealand's been a great performer over the last several years, but what if something goes wrong in New Zealand? What if we get foot and mouth disease, our economy tanks, and all our companies do poorly? Each country has its own risks, that's why you want some in Australia, some in New Zealand, Japan, the UK.

I think it's really smart for investors to be diversified right across the board. This is one that New Zealanders often get wrong. In terms of asset classes, we are dramatically over-exposed to residential property.

That's fine when residential property is going up, but there are a lot of people who have gone all in on property, and anything could happen – a government policy change, tax change, migration changes or even rising sea levels from climate change. We're also up to our eyeballs in term deposits, so you have a lot of people there with no protection against the impact of inflation.

Mark Lister – head of private wealth research, Craigs Investment Partners

---

HOBSON WEALTH PARTNERS HEAD of investments Mark Fowler is also a fan of diversification. Frankly, all of these money guys are. He says it smooths things out so that you don't come crashing down to earth with a thud. 'It means you'll never get the absolute highs, but hopefully you also don't get the absolute lows.'

For myself, I know that I'm a little lazy and I'm also a very small investor fish. I don't have hundreds of thousands to spread around, but I still know it's important to take this advice to heart. I want that hallowed 'diverse portfolio' – different shares from different types of companies, even from different countries.

Because I'm somewhat lazy, and actually not a great details person, I'm dead against picking individual companies to invest in myself. To do it right, I would need to be checking out their annual reports, watching their past performance and assessing where I think they're likely to go in the future. Even then, I would probably still get it wrong. Even the people who train in how to do that usually mess it up, but more about that shortly.

For me, I stick with index funds. They have very low fees, they give a great return and they split you across a bunch of different companies from the very start.

Funds, particularly index funds, are great because you don't need to know the difference between an income statement and a balance sheet. As I don't. You've strongly diversified what you're investing in, across hundreds of companies. Checking all of those balance sheets is now both impossible and unnecessary because you've spread your investment so far.

As I mentioned at the beginning, these chapters go in the order that I made these changes in my life, and that will probably work best as the order for other people too. I cut out overspending, committed to a budget, started saving, sorted out my KiwiSaver, then looked at investing.

That's because even when you're ready and prepared to jump in the sharemarket, it's not where you put every cent that you have – some in savings, some in KiwiSaver, some in shares. But how much in each? Well, that depends.

You need to think about your timing to figure that one out, or as the personal finance world calls it, your 'time horizon'.

YOU CAN THINK ABOUT three buckets in front of you, and say okay, well, how much am I investing that I won't need for the next five years? That's the proportion that goes into the growth bucket, which is shares and property investments.

The middle bucket is things that I might need over the one- to five-year frame. That goes into bonds, or fixed interest bucket.

Then you have the immediate needs, something that might only be invested for a month or two, certainly you need it within the next year. That goes into the cash or cash equivalent bucket, things like term deposits, your short-term investments.

Investors need to start by thinking about, why are they investing? What are the moments in their life that they're investing for and how far away are those moments? That's the first decision. The second decision, is what could go wrong? If the wheel falls off my car tomorrow, have I put everything into long term and I can't get money out quick enough to deal with it?

Hugh Stevens – chief executive officer, Smartshares

THIS IS DIVERSIFICATION AGAIN, but this time, it's diversification of money strategies, so that you have something ready for whenever life pulls a fast one.

Someone my age is likely to want to take on more risk and can reap the rewards of letting those riskier investments sit for a while. That's exactly what I'm doing; my main focus right now is investing into shares. I do it every single pay day. But I invest into more than one fund. I also have a cash savings account for emergencies. An investment in shares is not the same as your emergency savings fund. If something goes wrong in your life, at the same time as the sharemarket goes down, you will pay a big price for taking money out of there. I need both, but I have much more in shares.

Meanwhile, people heading into retirement these days could well live another 30 years. Typically, they're told to be more conservative with their money, because now is the time to enjoy the benefit of all that saving they did in their working life (I hope). As a result, term deposits or bonds are usually their main focus.

But when you're hoping to live another three decades in retirement, well, that's plenty of time for some money to be working harder for you in the sharemarket. Not most of your investments, because you're in a different life stage, but maybe part of them.

A rule of thumb that you will find floating around the personal finance space is to subtract your age from 100. What you're left with is what percentage of your investments should be high risk.

As I write this, I'm 30, so 70 per cent of my investments should be in higher risk things, like shares. When I hit 60, the thinking goes, only 40 per cent of my investments should be higher risk.

The problem with rules of thumb is that they don't apply to everyone, because we're all different. For instance, I'm what people call an 'aggressive' investor. I like to take a walk on the wild side of risk because I'm confident in my ability to ride out the lows without panicking, and I have the time up my sleeve to do so. My higher risk investments make up a bit more than 70 per cent right now, but certainly not up to 90 per cent. That's okay, that's just me. These rules of thumb are a useful place to start thinking about it.

Subtract your age from 100. What you're left with is what percentage of your investments can be high risk, as a rule of thumb.

The other thing you'll have noticed is that I like the index funds, which are part of a 'passive investing' strategy. You buy into the sharemarket as widely as possible and then you leave it alone. This is another thing that makes me more comfortable to ease into the aggressive, riskier funds. Because I did my research and saw that the average person makes the most money with the least effort from passive investing.

I don't argue with research. I take advantage of it.

There's been a lot of research done on active versus passive investment. The results show there's almost no point trying to be an active investor.

PASSIVE INVESTMENT IS BASICALLY when you try to buy into the entire market, whereas in active management you pick and choose which stocks, and how many of them, which is the 'weighting' of them in your portfolio.

People get sucked into trying to pick winners, but that's not how you become a good investor. You can't, over time, consistently outperform the overall market. Some people might win for a small time, but you can't do it consistently.

Dr Ayesha Scott – AUT

WHEN YOU BUY INDIVIDUAL companies, they could fall over. Who saw the Mainzeal collapse coming? Or Arrow construction? Not me. Individual companies keel over all the time. If you spread yourself around so that you basically buy every company in the economy, well, the entire economy is unlikely to keel over. Instead, it will probably keep selling things, keep employing people and keep sending you a piece of the profits.

Sam Stubbs is another person who's looked at the research and decided passive investing is the way to go. He founded KiwiSaver provider Simplicity as a way to provide low-cost funds that still made a good profit. Their team of industry professionals spent a year researching the best way to do this before they launched, and the evidence always came back to passive investing.

WINNING IN INVESTING IS not about being the hare, it's about being the tortoise. Everyone who looks into it sees that tortoises win, but it's not exciting. Our industry is built on getting you to make lots of transactions because you pay for that every time. But it's playing on your emotions. It's a way to get poor, not to get rich.

The richest people I've seen, in terms of ordinary New Zealanders, are the ones who stick a little bit of money in every week, and almost don't think about it after that. $20 a week ends up being $200,000 when you retire.

My advice to any young person would be just do it. Just get on with it. Do it in a way where you don't see the money leaving each week, and you don't have to think about it afterwards. That's the way to get rich.

Sam Stubbs – managing director, Simplicity

HUGH STEVENS FROM SMARTSHARES is yet another for Team Passive. He says it's not just that actively picking winners doesn't work. It's that you also have to think about how much more you're paying for the fund manager to pick those winners; and paying more eats into your profit or return.

OVER TIME, ACTIVE MANAGERS have not been able to out-perform the average market performance. But it's not what you expect, that argument, so it's very hard for investors to believe it.

If you think about the fact that the average investment in a balanced portfolio could be expected to earn 5.5 per cent a year, on average over the long term. Then take away a third of that in tax, take away 2 per cent for long-term inflation, you're left with something like a 1 or 2 per cent return.

So, if you're being charged more than that in fees, then you're going backwards. At that point, it doesn't matter how good the investment manager is.

That's why fee transparency is so important. You can lose all your returns on fees. And people are realising this – that maybe they really do have a great active manager who beats the market by 1 per cent, but they're charging 2 per cent in fees. Then what's the point?

Hugh Stevens – Smartshares

THE DIFFERENCE BETWEEN FEES might not seem like a lot, but just as you're wanting your returns to compound and snowball over time, this difference in fees will also compound over time. It eats into your return, taking a bigger bite year by year.

Read the fine print on fees, because there are a couple of different places you can be charged. Some places will charge you every time you buy or sell. Most will charge you a percentage of the money you have with them. Some will charge you a success fee. Make sure you know where they're charging you. There are lots of options. You don't need to take the one that charges you if you so much as sneeze.

But that's okay, you say, I'm willing to pay for results.

In 2010, a study published in *The Journal of Finance* found that only the top 2 or 3 per cent of managed funds made enough money to earn more than they charged in fees. The other 97 to 98 per cent charged more than they earned.

Even if you decide to ignore the fees charged, index funds often beat managed funds on the raw income they bring in.

The Wall Street Journal published research in 2016 that found 'between 71 and 93 per cent' of US mutual funds (active investing) were beaten by the closest comparable index fund.

Are you in the top 7 per cent of financial minds? I'm not. Can you find the fund manager who's that top performer? I mean, they'll all tell you they are. Are they?

I'm not saying that these people managing the funds aren't incredibly smart. They are. But trying to pick winners and losers is beyond difficult, no matter how much smarts you throw at it. The market is a fickle beast, and while it's human nature to think we can beat it, we usually can't.

I know. Buying and selling, combing through company results or paying someone to do that for you, it all feels like you're doing something. Like you're taking control, doing the extra work to get the extra reward. But you're actually better off to do less, to be passive.

Index funds diversify away the idea of being able to pick a winner. Instead of trying to find the one that will beat the market (unlikely) you bet on the market itself growing and businesses overall making money (very likely). It will still go up and down, so you put money in there for the long term. Given long enough, say 10 years at a time, shares get you a great return on your money. As a cheap(ish) investment that you can set and forget, it's hard to beat.

Doing less doesn't seem like it would be the way to make more money. And yes, you shouldn't pick just one or two studies that can make your point. You should look at all the research that's been done and find what the big overall lesson is.

Ignore the impulse that doing more will earn you more money. Making good decisions at the start, and leaving your money alone, is the proven way to make big bucks.

A 2018 study by Bank for International Settlements did exactly this, comparing a bunch of studies on active versus passive investing, in order to see what the general trend was. They checked research from as far back as 1968, as recently as 2014 and everywhere in between. It all showed the same thing. Passive index investing made more money over a long time than active fund management. As always, the key ingredients are time, doing your research at the beginning, then leaving it alone to do its thing.

Maybe you want something really recent and from New Zealand? Okay then. Thc tail cnd of 2018 was a bit of a nightmare for the sharemarket, with values falling further than they had in a long time. Supposedly, this is the active manager's time to shine. Many of them say they'll show their value when the market falls and they save you from the worst of it.

How awkward then that in the last quarter of 2018, as the market fell, it was the passive funds that came through the best. The entire market fell by 5.8 per cent, so that's the average that the active managers needed to beat. But data from NZX-owned

New Zealand sharemarket movements, Q4 2018

Smartshares NZ Dividend	-0.74%
Smartshares NZ Mid Cap	-2.49%
AMP Capital RIL NZ Shares	-4.70%
Smartshares NZ50	-5.34%
Simplicity NZ Share	-5.38%
Smartshares NZ Core Equity	-5.56%
Mint NZ SRI Equity Fund	-5.60%
AMP NZ Shares Index	-5.68%
AMP Capital Prem PUT NZ Shares Index	-5.75%
S&P NZX50 Index	-5.77%
Russell NZ Shares	-6.00%
Harbour Advanced Beta	-6.11%
AMP Captial NZ Shares	-6.21%
ANZ OneAnswer NZ Share	-6.74%
Summer NZ Equities	-6.96%
Forsyth Barr NZ Equities	-7.28%
BNZ Australasian Equity	-7.47%
Fisher NZ Growth	-7.62%
Milford NZ Equity Wholesale	-7.67%
Fidelity Super NZ Share	-7.80%
Fisher Premium NZ Equity	-7.91%
Nikko Core Equity	-8.74%
Asteron NZ Equity	-8.75%
NZ Funds Dividend and Growth	-9.74%
Fidelity NZ Shares	-11.10%
Average Active Fund	-7.34%

Please note passive/systematic funds are highlighted. All returns are net of fees but before tax for the period 01/10/18 to 31/12/18 inclusive. Source: Morningstar/Smartshares

Smartshares from the last quarter of 2018 shows that nine funds beat the average. Two were active. The other seven were passive.

Meanwhile, 15 funds did even worse than the average – 14 of them were actively managed.

SUPER AWKWARD.

Another unexpected place where you find evidence for this is the investing gender gap. Research shows fewer women have the confidence to invest, but those of us who do take the plunge tend to do better than the guys.

It's not because of mystical vagina powers, but simply that women tend to invest and then leave it alone. The researchers blame the difference on men 'trading' more, meaning that they shuffle their money around between different investments. Presumably, the guys are moving their money around based on their research about who's doing well and what they think is a good bet. It's a mistake that comes from a good place, but it is a mistake nonetheless.

Because of all that extra activity, a fascinating piece of 1998 research published in the academic journal *SSRN* found that, on average, men miss out on an extra 1.4 per cent return per year compared to women. Given that we've already talked about compounding, and about how a decent return is about 7 per cent, and an average one is around 5 per cent, that's a big chunk out of your money.

Hey, if you have the time and the knowledge to pick out, vet and monitor individual companies, and you're okay with the knowledge that all that extra work probably means you'll do worse, go for it. Personally, I'd rather spend my weekend sleeping in.

If you're worried about diving straight in then you can play around with the training wheels on. Give virtual trading a whirl, where you 'buy' shares with credits and track it as if you'd really bought it. The NZX runs one version (virtualtrading.nzx.com), which is nice because it's focused on New Zealand. Or you can use Investopedia's simulator for the American version (www.investopedia.com/simulator).

Virtual trading lets you figure out how it operates and get ready to try the real thing. It takes away the scary mystique by showing you most of it isn't complicated – or, at least, that you can avoid the complicated options.

Just don't play there for too long because the best thing you can do is just start. There are lots of places to start, and I'm not going to endorse any one option because what worked for me might not be right for you. However, a few good places for learner Kiwi investors to look are: the NZX's Smartshares, which has a payment plan where you can get into index funds for about $50 a month; Sharesies, where you pay as little as $5 for a variety of index funds and individual companies; and InvestNow, which has a range of managed and index funds that are relatively cheap to access. I've also seen people rave about the funds available through SuperLife, and the non-KiwiSaver funds at Simplicity are good if you want a cheap index fund that's thought about ethical issues.

There are so many options. You just need to look.

The average person can and should make investments to protect our future. We want to get the biggest bang for our buck without it turning into a second job or getting ripped off while we're not looking. We still have other stuff to do, like make dinner, turn up at work, and try to exercise once a month.

Embrace the fact that the lazy way is also the best way to make money. How often does that happen in life? There's no need to make this harder than it is. Most of us simply need to get on and do it.

Now, you may still want someone to hold your hand. And if you think you're the type of person who will panic when the market goes down and want to yank your money out even if you logically know you shouldn't, then maybe having a fund manager or financial adviser to work with is a good thing. But you should still know to focus on what fees are being charged. You should still know that a passive investing strategy earns more money for most people. Choose the option that works best for you, but just make sure you have all the information in front of you when you do.

Whatever you choose, it all works best when you think long term. Personal finance boffins will constantly drum into you the need to think in years or even decades. Just like flexing a muscle, you can build up your mental strength on this. Then when it starts working and you get better returns, it gets easier and easier.

The other side of the passive investing is something I've already talked about – you need time and lots of it. There's a well-worn saying that people use all the time because it's true: it's not *timing* the market, it's time *in* the market.

Timing the market is when you try to figure out when things are at their lowest and highest values, so you can buy lots when values have fallen. The plan is to then sell when they pick back up again. Supposedly, you make bank by pocketing the difference in value. Except you don't have a crystal ball, even experts struggle to do this, and most people who try will lose money. That's why so much of the 'active' investing strategy fails.

The other downside of timing is that some people are sucked into waiting for the 'perfect' moment to invest. That simply means you lose more money than you would make if you just got going, because you're waiting on the sidelines and missing out on the returns in the meantime. Study after study has shown timing the market doesn't work, particularly if you're a regular individual trying to do it. Frankly, it sounds like too much effort anyway.

OF COURSE, IN A perfect world we would buy when prices are low and sell when they're high. Keep doing that and you'd get very rich. The problem is, you can't. You don't know, at the time. You don't know whether it's going down further or whether you've caught the bottom.

You might get lucky once or twice, but more often than not people who try these tricks get it wrong and do more harm than good. I don't think you want to fall into the trap of betting the farm on things here at this specific point in time. For most people, you just need to take a long-term view and ride out the good and the bad.

I really like instalment investing – a steady investment, every week, every month, every quarter, whatever. That's effectively what KiwiSaver is. You're taking all of that timing out of the mix. You're buying while the market's going up, while the market's going down, you're buying high, you're buying low, and on average, you'll be somewhere in the middle. It's a much more sensible strategy.

When you take the guesswork out of it and do it automatically, you end up picking up some bargains. The lesson is just have a disciplined plan and stick to it. The biggest risk for a lot of people is not sticking to their plan. They have a financial plan that we know will work long term, but they either get distracted or panic in a rough period.

Investing is not rocket science. But the more we try to overthink things and pick where markets are going, the more we run the risk of making bad decisions.

Mark Lister – Craigs Investment Partners

TIME IN THE MARKET means you think in the long term, pick what you believe are solid investments and then leave them alone. You might pick one or two duds, but mostly this approach shields you from overhyped nonsense that will lose you money. I put my money into things that will keep earning money, so that I never need to sell them. For example, with shares, I personally like a fund with a high dividend payout.

This is a reason why I personally use a strategy known as 'buy and hold'. It's an extension of the passive investing strategy, which I use along with instalment investing. I've got an automatic payment set up for each pay day, going into an investing account. I then split that money across a few index funds, depending on how I'm feeling that day.

At first it was $100 a month. Some people will think that's a lot, others will laugh at the measly amount, but it was a lot for

Buy and hold A strategy of passive investing – buying investments and holding onto them long term, no matter what the market does in the short term.

me at that point. I had fun splitting that $100 each month across different index funds: $20 into the top 50 NZ companies, $30 into the top 20 Australian, the NZ Property Fund is paying good dividends so a whole $50 in there today.

I was investing my money for the future, but it felt like spending on something fun. Don't forget, I'm a spender whose money burns a hole in my pocket. Investing actually came easier to me than saving an emergency fund, because I felt like I was buying something fun. I looked forward to the day after pay day because it was the day I could have a play and buy some shares.

Buy and hold means you don't have to wait for your investment to shoot up in value and then time the sale of it just right. It means you don't pay a bunch in fees by constantly buying and selling. It means you don't spend all your free time trying to work out what the next hot investment is and hope that everybody else has missed it.

Avoiding all of that nonsense is important, but the most important thing to me is that it protects me from how damn emotional people can be. It's as much of a mental game as anything else. Research has found you feel the impact of a loss so much more than a win. Maybe you win three times and lose one, but that one loss will hit you hard emotionally. When we were living in caves, that's how we would remember not to do something dumb a second time. But we're not cave dwellers anymore – and you need to understand that impulse so that it doesn't control you.

I've watched people close to me make seriously dumb money decisions based on emotion. I know we're all capable of it, so I'm determined to not be the next victim.

You might think that won't be you. You might nod along sagely as people talk about the importance of thinking long term. You might have decided you're ready to ride the rollercoaster in the short term in order to make gains in the long term.

The problem is that people tend to agree with all of that, right up until they're tested on it. Then the sharemarket goes backwards (as it does from time to time), KiwiSaver goes down or property gets some new legislation whacked on it that sends everything backwards. People start talking about selling, or changing their KiwiSaver provider.

I've talked to plenty of people who confidently believed they were immune to the panic of emotion. They then lost money when they fell into exactly that trap. If you let emotions rule the day, you will buy when hype has reached fever pitch and prices are high. Then things hit a rocky patch and people sell out when prices are low. You're better prepared if you're more realistic and build in safeguards against your own emotions from the beginning.

I drip feed my money into the market, no matter what it's doing, and I don't look at the value of my investments when it's getting a little rough out there. I check in maybe once a month, sometimes once every few months. Some people only look every year or so.

What you don't want to do is look every day and freak yourself out when you see normal market ups and downs. And you definitely don't want to be keeping a close eye on it when the whole economy is having a bit of a rough time. Economies do that, and if everything is down at the same time, it's no big deal. Don't look. Go buy yourself a coffee. Let the market do the things that it does.

Authorised financial adviser Martin Hawes also uses buy and hold for his investments. He says he only cares about finding good assets, and then holding onto them. 'It's the antithesis of trading. Trading is taking a profit, short term, buying and then flicking. People can make it sound great when they talk about their successes, but they rarely talk about their failures. It's very difficult to do consistently.

'Buy and hold, on the other hand, is for the long term. Buying a good business at a fair price is much easier, and in the long run, much more successful. What's the long term? Well, often five years, with property maybe even longer.

'People tend to think of shares as very volatile and very risky, and they are volatile. But when I look at buying shares, I simply think, is this a business that I want to own? It's a quality mindset, and then just holding it for the profit. That's really what buy and hold is about.'

Hawes says his own biggest investing mistakes have always come from selling too soon. Now that he focuses on buy and hold, it doesn't mean he puts off selling forever and never getting the profits from an investment. He goes in from the beginning with a different mindset, which includes a plan for return throughout the investment's life.

That's why I have a big focus on dividend returns for my shares. I am not planning on those investments going up in value, although that would be nice when the day eventually comes that I sell. What I am planning on is them earning me money now, money I can reinvest. Compound, baby.

When I started learning about shares my husband was all for

it. We were in our late twenties and finally getting to the point where we had some disposable income for the first time. We wanted to set ourselves up for the future, so shares looked good. Then we chose different paths.

I knew I loved index funds, which the research showed I would do well in, that I would drip feed money in over time and then leave them alone. Ben was confident he knew which companies he wanted to invest in directly.

Even though I research personal finance and spend a lot of my time talking to financial experts, my husband has seen all of my previous money mistakes. He's spent years watching me do exactly the wrong thing on a daily basis. So do you think he wanted my thoughts on index funds? On diversification versus trying to pick winners? Nope.

The problem is that picking individual companies makes people feel clever and like they're doing investing 'properly'. You can tell people the opposite until you're blue in the face, but it doesn't feel right. And damn, people just like to feel clever. Here's where I throw my husband under the bus and tell you how he fell for exactly that trap.

The first mistake was in how many companies he invested in: two. He went for a fish company and an insurance company called CBL Insurance. He did his research, checked out the companies and then bought in. It looked good. He's genuinely very good at financial research. But it would soon go horribly wrong. These things can definitely go wrong, so let's talk about that.

11.

What goes up, must come down . . . and back up again

YOU MIGHT HAVE NOTICED a running theme in that last chapter – investing is a long game. Whether we're talking shares, property or whatever else you're into, you will make the best decisions when you're thinking a few years or even decades ahead.

You might have also noticed that I like shares. They're a good fit for my current stage of life, and I've sunk plenty of money (my version of plenty of money, anyway) into index funds.

I love them. But I also know that some years, my shares will go down. I also know that, even though it's the best place to grow my money, it's not gambling. I will not double my money in a year. Investing is not all or nothing. You're growing your wealth, the same way I grow my vege patch. You need to remember the tomatoes won't ripen overnight and every garden gets bugs sometimes. It's important to set realistic expectations about returns and think about how you'll handle bumps in the road.

I've braced myself for the reality that everything that goes up, must come down. I'm going to spread myself around quality investments, then ride the up . . . down . . . back up . . . back down . . . and up we go again. If I drew a line between those ups and downs, you would see it still goes up over time. The general rule is that the sharemarket goes up seven years out of 10 – so, the majority. But the three years it goes down might be hard and you need to make sure you don't bail out at exactly the wrong time.

Mark Lister is head of private wealth research for Craigs Investment Partners. It's a job title I've always loved, literally announcing to the world that he's the top guy to get other people wealthy. Yet, as he'll freely admit, even he has had investments go wrong.

'Any investor, whether professional or non-professional, will have plenty of stories about not getting their timing right. When you think about investing, there are lots of sensible things you can do to ensure you have a good experience and you do well over the long term. But over the short term, markets are completely unpredictable.

'I bought my first house in 2007, right at the top of the market. Within a couple of years, its value had gone down so far I'd nearly wiped out my deposit. Now, houses aren't a bad investment, but I had a terrible time with my first house. It was okay in the long term, because I waited until 2014 to sell it, but you really do have to wait out the cycle. The worst thing I could have done was panicked and tried to sell immediately.

'No one has a crystal ball that works perfectly. If anyone tells you they do, or thinks they do, that's your first sign to run a mile.'

That's why being a 'good' investor is not about picking the right stock or getting that one golden investment. It's about regular, disciplined investing. How boring, I know. But when the advice works, you don't need to cover it in flash and sizzle. It just works.

This is where we talk more deeply about the relationship between risk and return. If you want more money coming back to you overall, you have to put up with those 'riskier' investments. Except it's not risk like how we mean in normal, everyday life. Let me explain.

Being a 'good' investor is not about picking the right stock or getting that one golden investment. It's about regular, disciplined investing.

AUT crunched the numbers for the entire existence of New Zealand's sharemarket up to 2012 – a total of 114 years. Over that time, shares gave an average return of 10.75 per cent a year. Yes, that average includes the disastrous 1987 crash. It's a pretty incredible figure – my own personal rule of thumb is that anything over 7 per cent is decent.

Yes, the price to be paid for a good return is a rollercoaster in the short term.

That's why people talk about risk as a sliding scale for investments. You can use 'risk' to mean 'volatility'; that things will go up and down, and be a little unpredictable. But that's all short-term stuff. That's why the personal finance world is obsessed with time. Because over the long term, shares aren't all that risky, while a savings account might be.

David Boyle used to work at the Commission for Financial Capability, and is now with Mint Asset Management. It gives him a good overview of both the public and private sector aspects of looking after your money. He says that too much money sitting in a savings account means you're missing opportunities.

'People tend to assess risk based on what they see, but what they don't see is the buying power of their savings slowly being taken away. You can use the very simple analogy of lolly bags. If you got a fifty cent mixture fifty years ago, well, that's very different to what you would get today.

'You don't see that loss, you don't see inflation silently eating away at your savings account in the bank. But it's not delivering a return that you will probably need if you want to be able to look after yourself. As you get older, you'll need that money for things like looking after your health. Whereas, you can see every loss and gain in a managed fund, but the returns are usually bigger. You just see all of it, there in front of you.'

YOU MIGHT THINK YOU'RE taking a very low risk approach by putting all of your money in term deposits. Let's say you do that with all of your savings, from thirty years old. You might get a 3 per cent return per year. Take tax off that, it's only 2 per cent. Inflation is often more than that 2 per cent, if costs of living go up by more than that, then you're going backwards. You're not keeping pace with the cost of living. That's why, when you're thinking long term, cash and term deposits are actually a terrible idea.
Mark Lister – Craigs Investment Partners

IT'S FUNNY IN NEW ZEALAND, because we're a country full of entrepreneurs, where people love to set up their own business and go for it. Yet for some reason, the sharemarket freaks people out. I put that down to people not really knowing what the sharemarket is or not having much to do with it in daily life. A share is just a little piece of a business, and when you buy one, you get a little piece of the profits back.

Sure, businesses fail. But plenty more don't. That's why the experts bang on about diversification; if you've put $20 into a fund with 50 companies, and only 30 of them make a profit, that's fine. You're about to get some cash in the hand.

You don't need everything firing up at once, but spreading yourself around makes it more likely that something will be firing at different points. The airline does well one year, the next year it's a building company. If you buy quality, and lots of different types of it, then it makes it more likely that something will be firing up every year. Keeping a stream of money coming in all the time. That's what you need.

'Risk' in investing is different to how the rest of us use that word in everyday life. In normal life, I don't take risks. I'm a massive nana. I eat my vegetables, I look both ways before crossing the road, I read and obey the sign that says 'Danger: do not cross this fence'. In those cases, risk means don't do it. I don't do risky things. I like my chilled out life.

But in investing, risk is a sliding scale, and doing nothing at all has a risk of its own. If I want to look after myself both now and in 30 years, I need to take calculated risks. That's the difference. I understand the investing risk I'm taking and how I'm handling it.

IF YOU LIST ALL the risks, you may as well put in that we might get hit by a meteor, or the markets might crash, something might happen. Those are risks, but looking just at those can dilute the other risks. You can put your money under a mattress, and that's risky because someone might steal it. Or it stays there, but in twenty years when you try to spend it, you don't get much for it.

So when you talk about risk, you need to think about 'now risk', and 'later risk'. When you put money in shares and your now risk is high, if you want that money back in a week then that's a lot of risk. But the later risk is good, the longer you leave that money in good quality stocks, your later risk is a lot lower.

Turn it around the other way, and the now risk of putting money in the bank is zero or very little. But the later risk is phenomenal because the buying power is going down.

David Boyle – Mint Asset Management

WHEN YOU LOOK AT it that way, you realise the long-term picture is totally different from the now picture. In the sharemarket, across a bunch of investments, you may or may not lose some money. You will probably make some. But in a savings account, you will definitely lose money over time because a dollar is worth a little bit less every day.

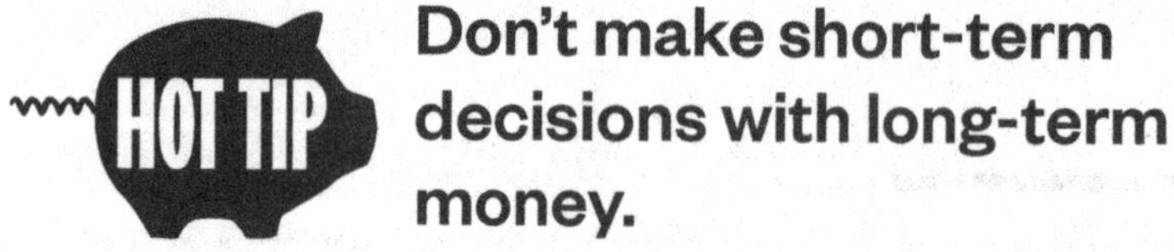

Don't make short-term decisions with long-term money.

I'll be better off in the long run by investing. In fact, for all the debate over various investing strategies, a bit of 2012 research by Charles Schwab found that between 1926 and 2011, if you held any regular investment for 20 years, it always produced a profit. There were different strategies that produced different levels of profit, but a 20-year holding period never produced a negative result.

Within that time, you need to be prepared to grit your teeth through some years where your money goes backwards. You just need to understand how risk and return work, and then turn them to your advantage.

YOU'LL GET THE BEST returns if you have lots of shares in your KiwiSaver. But the downside of shares – we call them more risky, but it's only risk in the volatility sense – is that they go up and down a lot. What you don't want is to find your portfolio is well down just at the time when you want to take money out.

A good way to think about it is that you get paid for taking on risk. Nobody would buy shares if they didn't give better returns. They do give the best returns, but you have to give them time.

Martin Hawes – Sumner Investment Committee

THAT'S WHY I TALKED about paying off debt and building up an emergency savings fund before we got to the investing. There's an order to these things and there's a very good reason for that order. You need to be secure and have the short-term situation sorted before starting on the long-term.

There are other things to be wary of, too. Like everything involving money, there are those who would like to scam you. The old rules are true; if it looks too good to be true, it probably is. There are no get-rich-quick schemes, so stay away from anyone promising that.

Martin says you should be wary of anyone promising you returns of 20 per cent or more. If the person tries to pressure you, be doubly cautious. If someone claims 'insider information' or uses a phrase like 'this investment's for the wealthy, but I'm able to open it to you on this occasion,' they're almost certainly bad news.

An approach from a stranger? Almost always a scam. Legitimate investment schemes will wait for you to do your research, then come to them.

Martin says you can expect about a 10 per cent return on shares over a period of time, if you're going for a growth strategy. So one year it might be 5 per cent, another it might be 15 per cent. It averages out to something pretty decent.

You shouldn't get overwhelmed by fear and just decide it's all too hard. After all, using that logic, we might just hide at home all day every day. Why try to get a job when you might get fired? Why leave your home when you're at risk of being run over?

A certain amount of risk is a reality in all parts of life. You just need to be prepared, calm and on the alert. Look both ways, then cross the road.

The Financial Markets Authority (FMA) knows this all too well. They spend their time trying to protect us from ourselves, stamping out the scammers before they have a chance to suck in too many of us. Because when you're trying to make a buck, the lure of finding the golden ticket is hard to resist.

Rules of thumb all investors should remember

- ! The promise of high returns with no risk? That's what's called 'too good to be true'.
- ! They don't give you anything in writing? Major red flag.
- ! It's a secret opportunity that only a few people know of and you should keep it to yourself? They're trying to stop you talking to others who might smell a rat.
- ! They offer you access to an overseas bank account, so that you don't have to pay tax? Stay away. You'll likely never get the money back.

Based on conversations with the FMA

THE TRICK IS TO never think that you're above being scammed. In my time as a journalist, I've covered plenty of court cases, or written about sob stories, where seasoned investors lost everything. In hindsight, all types of red flags were there, but a bit of knowledge can inflate your ego and your self-confidence, and make you feel immune to being scammed.

It's one of the reasons I've so far avoided cryptocurrencies like bitcoin.

At the risk of drawing the ire of all the tech fanboys, I don't trust cryptocurrency right now, and I'm likely to stay away from it for several years. This is despite the fact that I believe the hype. Crypto is a true disrupter, likely to change the way people do business in the same way the internet has changed so much.

But to be honest, I don't understand it well enough. I don't know enough about it to weed out those who are jumping on the bandwagon and those who have a good business case. I can't tell who's going to survive. I also can't spot the scammers lurking amongst the legitimate businesses, hoping to take advantage of the hype.

My own personal suspicion is that crypto is headed for a bubble similar to the dotcom one. Everyone became excited about the new digital future, internet companies sprang up all over the place through the late 1990s, before it suddenly came crashing down in 2001.

The digital revolution is still here, and companies like Amazon and Facebook are giants making a lot of money – but if I'd been investing in the 1990s, I wouldn't have known how to pick the winners. I wouldn't have known how to spot the scammers posing as revolutionaries, so I wouldn't have tried.

While we're at it, binary options can also get in the bin. If you start looking up investing terms online, you might soon find you're targeted with ads for binary options. They're an all-or-nothing type of 'investment', which I would actually call gambling or a scam. Stay. Away.

Another huge red flag is if an investment is based overseas. Even if you've done your homework and checked a company out, you want to double- and triple-check things before you send any money overseas. Once your money leaves New Zealand, there's nobody who can force them to send it back.

There's little that even the FMA, our money police, can do in that situation. Instead, an FMA spokesperson told me that Kiwi investors should ask companies if they're licensed or regulated in New Zealand. If they are, then at least you know you have legal options if things go wrong. If the person starts trying to change the subject or deflect your questions, that's a warning sign. You also don't need to take the person's word for it either – the FMA has a list of all businesses licenced in New Zealand, easily found on their website (www.fma.govt.nz). Ask the business for their information and then double-check it yourself.

Of course, if they're based in New Zealand and you think you've been ripped off, then you go back to the FMA. They're the ones in charge of helping you out.

There is investment and then there's outright gambling. Investing means you've done your homework, you're in it for the long haul and you make a series of decisions about how much risk you can stomach. You also spread your risk across different investments and different industries in case you get a dose of bad luck.

Gambling is doing little research, throwing money into something in the hopes of quick, high returns, and trying to get rich with very little work. Get-rich-quick schemes don't work. They leave you poorer than you started, just because you had a moment of greed and weakness. Don't fall for them.

Yes, shares give a great return over the long haul. They're also pretty easy to get into at my stage in life, certainly easier than trying to save up a deposit for an investment property. The trick is, you have to be in for the long haul, and I mean five to 10 years. When things inevitably take a turn for the worse, as they will, you have to hang in there.

All the experts say that if you panic and yank your money out, you're just cementing any losses. Calm down, take yourself to the pub for a commiseration beer and wait for things to get better in a couple of years.

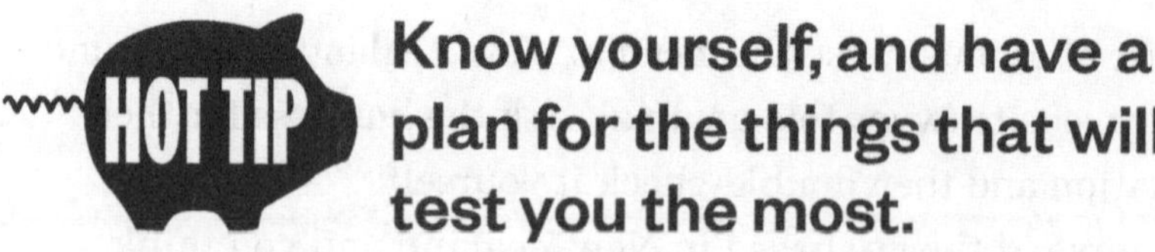

Know yourself, and have a plan for the things that will test you the most.

This is where you need to know yourself. I know my heart won't particularly like looking at my investments going backwards, even though my head knows it's normal. Plenty of us could become the person who panics and yanks their money out. I just honestly don't look. When I see the headline that the sharemarket is having a bad month, I take that as my cue to not look at my shares account or my KiwiSaver. No money is worth losing sleep at night. Know what you need to do and stick with it.

There's no point doing something that is a great idea from a textbook personal finance point of view, if it won't work for you. Your emotions can be the biggest danger to your money, so think about it ahead of time and be honest about how you might react.

In almost all situations, you should leave the money there. Market ups and downs, a company that hasn't done well this year but is still a good business, political posturing that sees business leaders get nervous – they're all normal and to be expected. You should have a plan in place for how you will handle that emotionally when it inevitably happens.

There are rare times when the situation is genuinely so bad, you just need to cut your losses. Maybe you didn't factor in market fluctuations from the start. Maybe the situation has got worse than you imagined it would. Maybe you bought into an individual company and it looks like it's about to go under.

As Kenny Rogers often reminds us, knowing when to hold them and knowing when to fold them is vital. And so we come to one of my favourite nerdy theories that you can apply to *everything* in your life.

It's called the Sunk Cost Fallacy. Basically, it means that when you've bought something, you psychologically want to get that money – your sunk cost – back. You don't want to admit defeat or admit a loss. When, actually, all you can do is cut your losses. Sometimes, that's the only way.

I have been insufferable since I've learned about this because I will apply it to absolutely anything. Say you're in a dead end job, going nowhere and feeling miserable about it. You might say you've spent five years there and need to find a way to get a promotion or it was wasted time. Well, your job has made it clear that *you're not getting one*. Rather than wasting another five years, start the new job hunt now.

You might be in a relationship that you know won't last, but you've been together a few years and maybe you could eventually change their entire personality? You won't. You could waste more time and emotional energy or you could call it a day and hit the dating scene again.

Or you might have invested in a company that's in absolute turmoil. You bought shares, and you don't want to sell them for less than you paid. You might come up with a clever plan to buy more while they're cheap, hoping you can make even more once it rebounds. Except there was a reason the company was in trouble and the whole lot folds. You should have sold for a pittance while you still could, but you wanted those sunk costs to pay off.

Sunk Cost Fallacy – it's human nature to feel like if you've put something in, you should get something back out. To be clear, this still only applies in rare cases, and I still use buy and hold almost always. Again, index funds protect me from most of this. But sometimes you just have to cut off the rot before it spreads. The beauty of humans is that we can learn and not get sucked in by our instincts every time.

So it is that we return to my husband, who dumped his investing money into just two companies. As many people know, sometimes the secret to a happy marriage is to step back and let someone make their own mistakes. I said my piece, then watched as my husband invested into the fish company and CBL Insurance.

At first, everything went great. The fish stocks in particular were going swimmingly (ba-dum-tish). They tripled in value, much to Ben's delight.

It took almost a year before the crash. Not the fish stocks, the other one. Suddenly, the news broke that CBL Insurance was in hot water with the Reserve Bank, having breached the central bank's orders by sending $55 million to overseas companies. The term 'liquidation' was getting bandied around a lot.

CBL's activities were even missed by the regulators for a while. This can happen from time to time. The best financial research can miss some shady practices. As you watch the company get into hot water, and the share price fall, you ask yourself: Do I cut my losses and get out now? Will the company go under completely? Or if I hang in there, will it recover? If I leave my money there, can I eventually make it all back?

As Mark Lister will tell you, there's no stock standard answer to that. Every situation is different, and you're going to have to do some more research to decide how you want to handle it.

BUY AND HOLD DOESN'T mean buy and forget. There's a big difference between saying you should stick to your plan and hold long term, and knowing that sometimes conditions will change.

When I bought my home and then values went down, well, it was still doing what I wanted it to do. I didn't buy it to make money, I bought it to live in. With shares, it comes down to what you bought it for in the first place. If it's a good quality share, and it's down just because the market is down, then you often won't need to do anything.

To think about the times you want to sell, you want to ask yourself, well, why did I buy this in the first place? Has the story, or the investment case for this business, changed? Is the management team not as credible as I thought? Would I still buy it today, if I didn't already own it?

The decision to sell is often a lot harder than the decision to buy. Because nobody wants to sell and crystallise the loss. You've not only locked in that loss, but you've got to admit that you were wrong in what you originally thought.

Mark Lister – Craigs Investment Partners

THAT WAS EXACTLY THE situation my husband found himself in.

'Should I sell the CBL shares?' Ben asked me, as we sat in a café where we'd seen the bad news in the newspaper.

'I wouldn't have bought into a single company in the first place,' I answered, because I can't ever resist a quick 'I told you so'. 'But now that you have, what do you think? Has the business story changed? Has the future of this company changed? Do you have confidence in them?'

Yes, the business story had changed. No, he didn't have confidence in them, he answered. He would sell the shares.

Too late. Before he had time to do anything, the money police stepped in and trading was halted on the shares. Nobody could buy or sell anything. We watched as interim liquidators were appointed by the courts. One investment company suggested shareholders might get back around 80 cents per share. A few months later, a new assessment put them at zero – worthless.

Ben had bought them at just over $3 each. He would get back less than a third of what he'd invested if he was lucky. He would probably get nothing.

He had made a few mistakes, which he will happily admit to those who ask. He hadn't bought enough companies to be properly diversified. Between the two that he'd bought, sure, the fish stock was going great. But the total collapse of the insurance company had pretty much neutralised those gains. All the experts recommend buying into far more than two companies.

No, he couldn't have predicted the company's collapse. It genuinely looked good when he first did his homework – and he did research the company properly, looking into its financial and business position. He has an eye for detail that I just don't. But there will always be things you don't see coming, and that's the very point of spreading yourself around. You're expecting the unexpected, so you'll do okay.

I'm not totally throwing poor Ben under the bus here; I'm sharing his story with his permission. He was irritated by the experience, but it was a lesson learned. Just like me, he's hoping that by being honest about his dumb money mistakes, maybe other people will avoid the traps.

He waited a couple of months to make sure he wasn't acting out of emotion, then sold the fish stocks. They were still doing great overall, but with the collapse of CBL Insurance, he was now only invested in one company. He had already learned the hard way about diversification. He decided he might as well sell out while they were on a high and jump into an index fund.

Maybe this is a helpful cautionary tale – or maybe I just wanted it on record that I was right and he was wrong. Hey, this is my book after all.

12.

My house became my castle

OF COURSE, RATHER THAN shares, many New Zealanders dream of the day they invest in their future by buying a house. You grow up, get a job and start saving for a house deposit – or at least, so the narrative goes.

I was never someone who cared too much about buying a house. It wasn't a big life goal for me. I figured renting was fine as long as you had a good landlord.

However, I ended up in a relationship with someone who saw it as a major life priority. So, fine, I figured it wouldn't hurt to buy a house. It was important to him, and it wouldn't be a bad idea, even if I had to knuckle down and save for a while.

Of course, as was usually the case before I overhauled my money relationship, my husband was the one who was right. Housing means stability and security. There are the nice lifestyle things, like knowing the landlord won't kick you out without notice, the ability to have pets and being able to grow a garden.

There's also the fact that it's an enforced savings plan; rather than paying rent forever, if you knuckle down and pay off the mortgage quickly, you should eventually have a roof over your head for nearly free. Your house is also an asset that means a bank will treat you differently if you want a loan for other investments. A house is really important for your wealth both now and in the future.

Housing means stability and security, and is an enforced savings plan. So it's important for your wealth now and in the future.

While the path to wealth is personal for everyone, Hannah McQueen says it generally involves getting a house, reducing spending and putting all the extra into paying down the mortgage fast. The reason she's such a fan of housing over everything else is that a paid-off house can be leveraged for other investments.

IT'S NOT THAT HOUSING specifically creates wealth. It's leverage that creates wealth.

Leverage is when you're using someone else's money to grow your own wealth. You can do that in business, where you use the capital of your investors to grow money; it's hard to do, success rate is low, but that is one way. The other, easier way is through property.

You come up with a deposit of 20 per cent, the bank gives 80 per cent, you get to keep 100 per cent of the gain. You've put in a little bit, leveraged off the bank, and you get to keep all the return.

It's not that property is amazing, it's that the relationship with the bank is amazing. I do say that with the disclaimer that not all properties are good and even, I'd say many properties are average to poor. But assuming you get a property that's not a dud, then you'll grow wealth.

In theory, the sharemarket performs better than property. Shares could get a 12 per cent return over a period of time, property might only get a 6 per cent return. So at face value, without leverage, shares make more money. But if you have $100,000, and you can put it into shares, or into property as a 20 per cent deposit, then you can buy a $500,000 property. While the return on that property is still 6 per cent, 6 per cent of $500,000 is more than 12 per cent of $100,000.

Hannah McQueen – EnableMe

YOU COULD USE YOUR home to get an investment property or buy a business. You already know I think it's smarter to get cash coming in, rather than constantly buying and selling to make money. Your home can be a valuable asset, sure, but it can also create opportunities to get money coming in, so it's worth being aware of the power of leverage.

Unfortunately, by the time my husband and I saved what would usually be a decent deposit, we were in the midst of a housing crisis. Average house prices were over the million dollar mark in Auckland, and the rest of the country was also shooting up in value.

To add more pressure to the situation, by then I'd realised just how misguided I'd been in not caring about buying a house. As well as everything else I've mentioned, most pensions – particularly New Zealand's scheme – are set up to pay your living costs. But they assume you'll have a paid-off home by the time you retire, so there's no budget for rent. If you're still paying rent or even still paying off your mortgage, you could end up blowing your entire pension just trying to keep a roof over your head.

Research from Massey University in 2018 showed the pension wasn't even enough to live a 'no frills' lifestyle, meaning no entertainment like heading out to the movies or travelling to see the grandkids. You can imagine how bad it could get if you're still having to pay to keep a roof over your head.

I had also, by then, had the realisation of how bad landlords could be. For much of my renting life, I'd had great landlords; they completed the major repairs, even if the minor ones were sometimes ignored, and mostly left us alone as long as we paid the rent. It worked great, and everyone was happy.

But your home is so central to your life that if you encounter a bad landlord, it can quickly become a nightmare. The last landlord I ever had was a true horror story, and they cemented my determination to get out of the rental market. Let's just say, you could shorten his first name to Dick, and we ended up calling him that a lot behind his back.

He owned a block of three properties and seemed fairly easy-going at first. But about six months after we moved in, he decided he wanted to make some changes to the properties and was clearly thinking about selling.

So far, so good. His properties – he could do what he wanted. When he turned up without notice to make repairs and do a spot of painting outside, I didn't say anything despite him giving us no notice that he was coming onto the property. I figured hey, it's just a few repairs. He wasn't the first landlord who had randomly turned up to do such work.

For the record, it's not cool to just turn up with no notice and it's illegal to come into the house with no notice. That law is meant to protect the fact that it's the tenant's home, and you should be able to privately relax in your home. But I put up with it, in the name of keeping things friendly.

Then one day, I was in the kitchen washing dishes. A shadow fell across me. I looked up to see the landlord at our front door, hands cupped against the glass, peering in.

I froze, shocked. He was literally peeping through our windows for some unknown reason. I was home alone on my day off. It occurred to me that it was lucky I was wearing pants.

Safe to say I made sure I was fully clothed at all times for the rest of the time I was in that house. No more pants-free Sundays. Who needs to relax in your own home, after all?

But it wasn't enough. A few weeks later, I stepped out of the shower and heard two unfamiliar, male voices. I froze again.

Then I realised it must have been a trick of sound. Nobody was home but me, so the sound must have been coming from outside.

I threw on my dressing gown and crept down the stairs of our townhouse, feeling silly. Only to jump out of my skin when I saw the landlord with an unknown repairman bent over our stove.

The landlord looked up at me, at least having the good grace to be startled.

'Oh!' he said. 'I thought you weren't home. We're just looking at the stove. He was right here, so I thought I'd just let him in, no need to bother you about it.'

Again, I was too shocked to do anything. I didn't have a response prepared because I'd never expected anything like this would happen. I was also incredibly conscious of still being damp from the shower, only wearing my dressing gown.

I felt vulnerable. I just nodded my head and crept back upstairs to get dressed, fast.

A few weeks after that, my husband caught the landlord peering in our windows again. He wasn't as quiet about it as I'd been.

There's a very real power imbalance when you're renting. You might need a reference for your next house or you might want to be allowed to stay in your current house when the lease comes up for renewal. The landlord might be a nightmare, but maybe the house is the only affordable one near your work.

Landlords have also been known to search the Tenancy Tribunal database for names, and refuse rentals to people who have been to the tribunal. Even if the renter was the one in the right, they're branded a troublemaker.

As a side note, there are people who can help you navigate

these tricky waters. Renters United is Wellington-based, while the Tenants Protection Association is Christchurch-based. If you're elsewhere in the country and need help, call one of them anyway. If you're based outside of New Zealand, look for your local renter advocacy group or citizen's advice. They're helpful, knowledgeable people.

All things considered, I was ready to make the sacrifices needed to save that home deposit.

Getting that first deposit is, to my mind, the hardest part. Often the mortgage repayments are the same as or possibly even lower than your weekly rent. It's just saving up that huge chunk of cash that will convince the bank to give you the rest. It's a killer.

David Boyle, the guy who used to work at the Commission for Financial Capability and is now with Mint Asset Management, is a KiwiSaver wizard. That's where he thinks you should start in saving up your house deposit; KiwiSaver.

Supercharging your KiwiSaver is an important first step in saving for a house.

KiwiSaver is a retirement scheme, yes, but you're allowed to break into it for your first home deposit. It's also a scheme that you can supercharge. If you're saving at least 3 per cent, then you'll get the employer contribution of 3 per cent and the yearly tax credit of $521.

Suddenly, you're not only having to save your own money. You're reaping the rewards of KiwiSaver incentives, which are doubling your money before you even get an investment return.

David says that's exactly what you need, if you're going to pull together that intimidating house deposit. 'I can't think of a better way to save for your deposit. Those extras make all the difference. Then you need to think about the length of time it will take to get you there. That's what will guide your decision, in terms of what fund you choose.'

IF YOU'RE EMPLOYED, GET at least that 3 per cent contribution so that your employer is matching you dollar for dollar. If you're not putting in to KiwiSaver and missing out on that, then you're really doing yourself a disservice.

You do want to think about how long you expect to be saving for. With KiwiSaver, we often talk to our clients about moving to a conservative fund if they're thinking about buying in the next year or so.

Rupert Gough – chief executive officer, Mortgage Lab

WE'VE TALKED ABOUT KNOWING your timeline and investing according to it. You don't want to lose everything if you don't have much time, but you don't want to miss out on returns if you do have time. As both David and Rupert point out, if you want to properly supercharge your retirement savings for a house deposit, you need to think about how much time you need.

Look at the average first home price in your area (check online or call some real estate agents), work out how much deposit you'll need (usually a minimum of 10 per cent, 20 per cent looks better to the bank if you can get it), and then work backwards to see how long it will take you to save.

Maybe you're stuck in an expensive place like Auckland or Queenstown and don't have the option to move somewhere cheaper. That might mean you'll be saving for five or 10 years, which is good and bad. It means you have the option of making your money work harder while you wait, with a little more risk to get better returns.

Maybe you're somewhere cheaper or you've been saving a while already. Everyone's situation is different, but many of the financial experts agree that if you plan to use the money within five years, you should keep it in a conservative fund.

David says you don't want a market downturn just as you were ready to put down a house deposit. 'Anything with exposure to equities needs a five-year minimum. And more than that if you're looking at a growth fund. You do want a bit of growth, but not to risk maybe 20 per cent of your balance if a correction occurs, something like that.'

You also definitely don't need to stop at your minimum 3 per cent KiwiSaver contribution – remember compounding, so every little bit you can save will help. Just make sure you're putting it somewhere that makes sense for how long you plan to save.

You could talk to payroll at your company and increase how

Equities Equities, shares, stocks — they're all the same. It's referring to the fact that when you buy a share, you own a little piece of that business.

much you're putting into KiwiSaver, or you could invest extra elsewhere yourself, looking at term deposits or shares depending on how much time you have. This is a good time to think about going to see a financial adviser who can help you to decide on a plan.

Pull every lever you have to get yourself over the line. Each little bit tips the scales further in your favour.

If you're in Auckland or some other expensive city, it's not easy, but there are options. You can look for cheaper housing, like an apartment or townhouse. You can move elsewhere, although that's not always possible depending on what you do for work, or because you want to stay close to family. Money is simply a tool to achieve quality of life, after all, and having your loved ones close by is huge for that.

David Boyle suggests an investment property in a cheaper city as another option, either to start building your leverage or maybe as somewhere you want to live in the future. It's a good point. Sure, you're based in Auckland now, but what if your family live up north and you'd like to move back at some point?

Well, then maybe you should save up a Northland-sized deposit, buy a place there and rent it out. Then you carry on living in Auckland, still renting yourself. I know someone who did that with a Tauranga house before Tauranga houses went crazy. That home would be worth a pretty penny now.

Just remember this strategy means you can't use your KiwiSaver; you can only break into your KiwiSaver for your first home that you will be living in – not an investment property someone else will be living in. This is just another reason to get your maximum benefits from KiwiSaver and then have other investments that you control yourself. It's good to have other money working hard elsewhere that you can use if you need it.

Mortgage Lab's Rupert Gough says you can also think about how big a deposit you want to save. There is a bit of flexibility. You can sometimes have only 5 per cent for a fixed-price building contract. But in most situations, 10 per cent is considered a low deposit, and 20 per cent will get you good treatment from the bank, including more willingness to negotiate on interest rates.

'If you can get to 20 per cent deposit, you will get a significantly better deal from the bank. We had a client who had saved up 17 per cent – they managed to get that last 3 per cent gifted to them, and it saved them $10,000 because the whole mortgage rate dropped by about 1 per cent.'

Once you've reached that home deposit goal, whether it takes months or years, take a moment to celebrate. Then prepare yourself for the next phase – convincing the bank that you're a good bet.

When it comes to negotiating a mortgage with your bank, don't forget it's just that – a negotiation. There is some prep work you can do to make yourself look like a good option, and squeeze a better deal out of your bank.

LENDERS ARE ALWAYS LOOKING to understand your financial position and how attractive you are financially. You need to have been saving up, you need a clear idea of your income and your outgoings. There is a little bit of flexibility in terms of what size of deposit a bank will accept, but not much, so you need to look really attractive financially.

Make sure you've paid down any debt, any outstanding bills. You can have some debt, but make sure it's clear you have it under control and you're paying it off. As part of that, a few months before you reach the application stage, don't take on any new borrowing, no new credit cards. You don't want to appear as someone who is credit hungry.

This sounds obvious sometimes, but you should show you've thought of the additional expenses that come with owning a home – the insurance, council rates, home repairs.

Check what it might look like if interest rates went up 1 or 2 per cent. We've had such a long period of low interest rates, some of us have forgotten that they're not here to stay. If the interest rates change, you need to know that you won't sink.

Jose George – Canstar

IF YOU ARE REGULARLY late paying your utilities bill, that can really count against you, whereas a few years ago that wasn't such a measured thing. The number of things that they look at, and the black-and-white tick-box mentality they take sometimes, it can make it more difficult for people who don't have their finances prepared.

It used to be they would expect you to change your habits once you'd bought the house, and live more frugally to pay for everything. But now they'll say to you, you're not showing great control with your money, you're getting Uber Eats a lot, so we're a bit nervous about what you'll do once you're in a house.

You need to be on your best behaviour at least three months before going to see the bank. You need to start on a good budget today, rather than planning to cut things out once you're in the house, or, at least, showing that you've made a really good effort at correcting things.

Rupert Gough – Mortgage Lab

Be on your best behaviour three months before applying for a mortgage. Live on a tight budget, pay off debt, and make sure you cut any frivolous spending.

IT CAN BE A minefield trying to figure out what the best rate is and who you should go with for a mortgage. Don't just stick with where you currently bank. Remember how compound interest means little investments snowball to become huge? Well, a tiny difference in interest rates between banks can snowball to be tens of thousands of dollars more over the course of a 30-year mortgage. Of course, I'm hoping you'll pay it off faster than that, but to help you do that, you need the best rate for you.

Most experts recommend only negotiating the interest rates, because those will have the biggest impact on how much you end up paying. Don't be distracted by little freebies, like the free TVs that were fashionable for a while. A TV is peanuts compared to what an interest rate will save you.

Canstar also has a mortgage calculator tool that you should check out (www.canstar.co.nz/compare/home-loans). I like it because it's easy, it compares all the banks and Canstar is independent, so you know they aren't trying to sell you something that doesn't actually work for you. If you're not in New Zealand, have a look around for a similar independent comparison. It will be around and it could save you thousands.

Jose says they created the tool because it's so important to do your homework, but people get overwhelmed. 'A lot of people just walk straight into the bank that they've always known. Whereas knowledge is strength and power, and you really need to know what's available in the market.

'Then think, do you want to take advantage of the short-term rates that are usually a little cheaper? Do you want to lock in a five-year deal, so that you have stability? Once you know how long you want, the term, then you can go and negotiate that with the bank.'

That's what people mean when they talk about how you 'structure' your mortgage. You don't just have to put it all on a five-year term. Personally, Ben and I decided to split our mortgage into three: one at a good two-year rate, one at a good one-year rate, one that is floating.

The idea with the floating is that, even though the rate changes and can be more expensive, you're not locked in to paying a certain amount. You can pay extra, but you don't have to. We keep it as the place where we put any unexpected windfalls, like say, an advance for writing a book. We can pay the mortgage off faster without being locked in to paying at a high rate all the time.

If I just got too advanced and lost you, that's fine. It took me a while to get my head around the mortgage language, and sometimes I think you only learn by jumping in and starting to do it. Do go and talk to a couple of mortgage brokers, even if you decide not to work with them. They can run you through these options and help you figure out what's best for you.

When we decided to save up our deposit, I was already starting to change my relationship with money. I was warned the bank would look at my spending history, and knowing this gave me the extra incentive I needed to keep clamping down on dumb behaviour. I put myself on a cash diet, taking out my spending money for the week, so that I would see it leaving my hands and not be tempted to overspend. Once it was gone, it was gone. There was also no paper trail for a cheeky café visit.

It took a while and, to be honest, it helped that my husband and I were able to pool our resources. Two KiwiSavers together add up to quite a lot. We also took advantage of every bit of help we could, like the KiwiSaver HomeStart grant you can get in New Zealand. The rules change a bit depending on how much you earn and how long you've been in KiwiSaver, but you can get up to $10,000. A big leg up. With all of that, we could scrape together a 10 per cent deposit.

We also had a bit of help. I'm reluctant to call us 'lucky' for this, but my husband was left some money after his dad died when he was young – so, not lucky really. But the inheritance took us over the line to a 20 per cent deposit. Let me tell you, I know the bank will treat you better once you get over that line. Get there if you can. Suck it up and make yourself look good in other ways if you can't.

So, we made it – to a little unit on the edge of central Wellington that was all ours. We escaped that pervy landlord. We didn't have to worry about the lease not being renewed or the house being sold from under us. The money we'd previously paid towards rent went into paying off our home and to a future where we would own the home mortgage-free.

As someone who'd never dreamed of home ownership, I was shocked by how different it felt. I knew the space was my own. I knew I wasn't going to step out of the shower to find some creep in my kitchen. I knew I could paint the dingy brown walls a beautiful bright white.

I told one of my friends of my surprise at becoming so emotionally attached. She laughed at me and said it was nothing compared to how she'd reacted to getting her own first place.

'I couldn't sleep for the first month,' she said. 'I just walked around at night, stroking the walls. I couldn't believe they were my walls.'

13.

Getting rich on paper doesn't make you rich

FOR ALL THAT I love about being a homeowner these days, there is a reason I've waited until this late in the book to talk about housing. The problem with buying a home is that people often mentally stop there. You get a roof over your head, you start to pay it off and some people will congratulate you as if you don't need to do anything else to secure your financial future. Uhhhh . . . Can you eat your house? Go on holiday or set sail to see the world on your house?

Getting a roof over your head and paying it off are very important for securing your future. If you don't have to pay for your living costs, your retirement will be a lot easier. But I imagine you'll also want to spoil the grandkids with Christmas presents, travel to see new places before your hips give out, and turn the heating on in winter. All of those things take cold, hard cash. I don't know about you, but I don't want to have to remortgage my home in my old age, or be forced to sell up and move to the middle of nowhere.

Even if you're more of a here-and-now type of person, you'll probably want to be able to look after yourself if your life hits the skids. If I get sick or finally say something dumb enough that I get fired, I need to have other investments that bring in some money.

Don't forget that when you buy a house you suddenly also have to pay rates, insurance (which is steep if you live in shaky cities like Wellington or Christchurch), and shell out for maintenance or repairs. For instance, right after buying our first home, we sprang a leak in the laundry. You don't mess about with water damage, so we simply had to take it on the chin. The repair was expensive and bit into our emergency fund – and that wasn't even a big problem.

The capital gains from housing can be good. A house will also give you access to leverage, cheap money that you borrow against your house to invest into other things like a business. But housing can go backwards, just like any other investment. It isn't a financial plan by itself.

The other big problem is a dangerous mindset that became

Capital gain The increase in what something is worth, which you only earn when you sell that thing. If you sell a house for more than you paid for it, that is capital gain.

particularly obvious around the time Auckland housing went crazy. People saw the value of their house going up and felt richer. Some gave in to the temptation to go out for dinner more, maybe to extend the mortgage based on their new house value so they could put in a pool, or booked an overseas holiday on the credit card – when, actually, their circumstances hadn't changed.

In a way, I get it. Between 2014 and 2017, average Auckland residential property values jumped 45 per cent. The average house in our biggest city was suddenly worth $1.07 million. For first home buyers, it sucked, but not for those who already owned a home. It's pretty difficult not to let a number like that go to your head.

You're only richer on paper though, and that's why this gets dangerous. It's the reverse of when shares go down and you only lose the money if you actually sell. Your house is only worth that much if you sell it and move somewhere cheaper. Are you actually looking to sell? Is your family in Auckland? Is your job tying you in place? If so, that price increase is meaningless to you.

There's an important difference between paper wealth and real wealth. If you're not planning to cash in by moving out of an overheated property market and into a cheaper region, it's meaningless. Paper.

WHEN PEOPLE THINK ABOUT their own circumstances, they do often confuse paper wealth with real wealth. So you buy a house for

$500,000, over time house prices increase to say $700,000, then in theory you are $200,000 richer. But that's unrealised, so it's paper wealth. The only time you get that gain is if you sell that asset. If you buy and sell within the same area, you're just transferring wealth from one property to the next.

When you think about real wealth, ultimately, are you getting payment or income from it? Or are you able to express that through a business or a productive asset. You might buy something like a bond, which pays you some fixed income regularly. That's tangible wealth, or real wealth if you like.

The key thing with paper wealth is exactly that; while on paper it looks good, there's potentially no cash flow. It might look good on your home spreadsheet, but that's it. Bear in mind, while we've had a prolonged cycle of values going one way, and it's quite some time since people can remember prices going the other way, ultimately that paper wealth can erode.

While we're at it, there can be an element of paper wealth with equity markets as well. You can have a non-dividend-paying, but high growth equity. The recent example would be Facebook, which went up very high, but recently lost 30 per cent off its value.

Mark Fowler – Hobson Wealth Partners

MARK SAYS IT'S A common trap for people to see rising prices around them and extend their own debt levels past what they can pay for. It's exactly that – a trap. 'If you have the belief that housing is a one-way bet, then you're in danger of over-confidence, and it can spill into how you approach other areas of investing. We always just try to highlight that things don't go up forever.

'In the past, sometimes property has gone down by 20 to 25 per cent. So you have people borrow to their limit to buy a house worth $500,000, and a year later it's worth only $400,000. Then you have negative equity.'

Negative equity? That's where you owe more to the bank than you can sell the house for. Basically, it would be a financial nightmare to sell. You're stuck either selling and walking away with no house and still owing the bank money, or holding on to that house even if you don't want it anymore. Let me tell you, as someone who has bought and sold a house; it's only ever worth what you can sell it for. You can get all the valuations and appraisals that you like, but in the end, you have to find someone who is willing to pay for it. It can be easier said than done.

Mark says that, basically, if you want to stay in the same region, you can't take advantage of rising house prices by selling your own home. 'If you have to buy back into that market, it could be very difficult if prices keep going up while you're on the sidelines. For selling a house, there's also things like transaction costs, so real estate agent fees and these types of things to consider.

'If you're exiting that market and going somewhere else, it's potentially a good opportunity. But ultimately, if your circumstances aren't changing, maybe not. It can be very difficult to get back in.'

While we're at it, the obsession with houses that are much bigger than we need irritates me. While we were looking for our first home in Wellington, and even the second in Hamilton, people warned us of the same thing over and over again.

'You need it to be three bedrooms, minimum. Just think of the resale value. You can't get as much when you sell a smaller house.'

That's sounds more like a pyramid scheme than an investment plan. There is so much wrong with that idea that it tends to reduce me to a malfunctioning robot when it's said to me in real life. There are so many ways to rebut it that I can't pick one, and end up stumbling around and changing the subject.

For starters, over a 30-year mortgage, you usually pay twice the price of your house. The interest in mortgage repayments typically ends up being about the same as your original purchase price.

If you buy a smaller house and have a smaller mortgage, you'll be able to pay it back at much more than the minimum rate. As soon as you do that, you wipe out tens or even hundreds of thousands in interest payments. I don't know how much capital gain you're planning on making, and nobody knows what the housing market will do in the future, but you can count on not having to give that extra interest to the bank. That's money in your back pocket. It might even be worth more than future capital gains.

I can work things so I guarantee I save tens of thousands in debt payments, or I can hope to maybe get tens of thousands when I sell. Bearing in mind that I'll probably be in the same market, and we've already talked about how difficult that will be. Which option do you think I like better?

The other thing is the assumption that people know what

future buyers will want in a house. You might sell your home in two years' time, or it might be 20. I'm willing to bet that housing trends change in that time. What happens if you buy a three bedroom home, use only one bedroom of it, then by the time you sell people have worked out small houses are great? Well, your hallowed resale value just went through the floor, didn't it?

This isn't a theoretical argument either. The New Zealand housing market proved my point in 2018. The July 2018 Quotable Value House Price Index shows that while most of the market went flat, with prices not going up or down, for the 'affordable' (read: small and cheap) end of the market, it was still running hot. The tide is already turning for people to prefer smaller houses.

Not to mention the fact that rates, power bills, insurance, everything is cheaper when you have a smaller house. Hey, if you need a bigger house, get one. But do you need one or do you want one? Worse, do you feel like you 'should'? Personally, I'm not gambling such a big investment trying to guess what some mythical person in the future will pay top dollar for.

That said, I've still included housing in this book, because you can use property to significantly improve your financial position. As with most things in life, you need a mixture of working hard and luck. The harder you work, the more you tip the scales in your favour.

When my husband and I were finally in a position to buy our first home, we were in Wellington. That was part of the reason we were able to do it; until then we'd been based in Auckland and, at that time, there was no way we could have afforded something in the Auckland region.

Every single weekend for about six months, I went to multiple open homes. I'm not kidding. It was my life for that six months. Two open homes on Saturday, three on the Sunday, get home Sunday evening and scratch all of them off the list of possibilities.

Our budget was tight, like most first home buyers, yet we had certain things we wouldn't compromise on. It didn't need to be flash, but we wanted to live in a place that actually felt like a home. We were prepared to do minor cosmetic renovations, but not take on a place that was falling apart, because we didn't have the expertise to know if it would become an expensive mistake.

Finally, by December, we found it. It was a little unit, immaculately presented, precariously perched on a cliff above native bush, and just close enough to the city that I could walk to work. It was in a pair of units with another house directly above us. The place needed a repaint, but that was a minor issue. We went back and forth in the negotiations, trying to lowball the sellers. The final price was at the very, very top of our budget.

We dithered, then signed on the dotted line.

We took over the house in January, and that first evening we ate takeaway pizza on the floor while marvelling at the fact we'd bought our own house. Four walls to call our own. A view over the harbour, where you could watch the rain lash down on a typical dramatic Wellington day.

By February, only a month later, we were feeling relieved we'd made the decision to go right to the edge of our budget. Auckland's housing madness had started to spread and it hit

Wellington hard. Prices climbed steeply. We breathed a sigh of relief that we'd accidentally hit it lucky.

We painted the walls a fresh, stark white, and debated whether we should redo the laundry. Every now and then we looked at online house valuations and laughed at it climbing.

It's strange, being on the other side of the housing crisis. You spend so long struggling to build up a deposit that can keep up with the prices. Then you're in and (hopefully) watching your own values go up. I understand how it can go to your head. But it didn't really matter to us because we weren't going anywhere.

Then a minor miracle happened. I'd been campaigning for a new job for about a year, running NZME's podcasts. I knew I could do the job, it was just a question of whether the company wanted to allocate the resources needed to do podcasts properly.

Finally, they decided they did – but they also wanted me to come to Auckland to do it.

I knew there was no way we could afford Auckland, at least, not with the quality of life that I wanted. I negotiated a compromise. I would be based in Hamilton, but make sure I was in the Auckland office for part of the week, every week.

I won't lie, it took a few more months of negotiating. If you want something out of the ordinary, you'd better be prepared to patiently argue your case and stick to your guns. But I knew what I wanted, and why it was worth it for both sides. Eventually, they went for it.

Now was the time to seriously think about that rising value of our house. By then, we'd been in it for almost three years. We brought in a few realtors to hear what they thought we could get.

It turned out our house had gained almost as much in three years as my husband and I had earned in our jobs in that time.

It was a crazy realisation. Even those online valuations had underestimated our house, because of course they hadn't taken into account the minor improvements we'd made.

Also, our place was the little house everyone had warned us against. It had been just perfect while we'd lived there, with as much space as we needed, and the mortgage repayments were low enough that we didn't have to bring in a flatmate. We could have privacy and invest a little into making it nicer.

By the time it came to selling, it was one of the few properties considered at the 'affordable' end of the scale, and it was neat as a pin. We brought a builder through to put together a report, and he called us afterwards trying to get it for his daughter before it went on the market. Because it had high competition, it pushed the price up.

We'd accidentally timed things perfectly. We couldn't have deliberately tried to do it, and I wouldn't ever try. I watch the housing market as part of my job, and I still didn't know that we were buying right before prices would go crazy. I didn't know I'd get a job opportunity that would mean we would sell when the market was high and move to a more reasonably priced area. You don't have a crystal ball that lets you time the market accurately, and anyone who tells you they can predict what's going to happen next is either stupid or trying to scam you. You need to learn how things work, so that you can make the most of every bit of luck you get.

Even if you get a dose of good fortune like we did, you can squander those gains if you're not careful. We took a deep breath, calmed each other down and planned our budget for our unexpected windfall. We wanted a modest family home in Hamilton, but it didn't need a swimming pool. We did want it to be a nice place where we could bring friends around and not feel embarrassed about holes in the wall.

We ended up, once again, with a small house that was just big enough for our needs. It is three bedrooms now because we might have kids in the future and we don't plan to move for several years. But the bedrooms and the living space aren't enormous. Because it's smaller, we could afford a place with a garden where I have my beloved vegetable patch, a pristine white kitchen that makes my heart sing, and in a part of town where I can cycle to work.

You can have anything you want, but not everything at once. I'm so happy with the choices we made. Who knows, if we do have kids, maybe a smaller house will force them to spend time with us.

As with most things in life, we got ahead through a mixture of luck and working hard. I was lucky to have bosses that believed in me and were (eventually) willing to be flexible about where I was based. I was lucky enough that my husband was also able to move. I was lucky enough to marry someone who loves a bit of DIY – and is actually good at it. We were extremely lucky that the housing market went in our favour.

We worked hard by deciding to base ourselves in Hamilton because it was close to Auckland, but cheaper, and it was where my husband's family lived. I was willing to bite the bullet and be away from home for part of the week. I proved to my bosses that I was worth the investment by producing good podcasts for

18 months with little help and working quite a bit of overtime. We were willing to live in a modest home and put in the elbow grease to make it much nicer.

The end result is a mortgage we could pay off in about 20 years – maybe less – at current rates, all while still being able to go out for brunch on the weekends. I'll take living the good life over rattling around in a house that's too big for my needs, thanks.

I made compromises to increase my quality of life. I would happily make all of these decisions again. I did my research, weighed up my options and went into this with my eyes open.

On the other hand, I know people who moved to the regions for a cheaper home and then felt trapped – people whose jobs prospects stalled, who were isolated and away from the people who loved them. They made a move for cash and it didn't work.

What is the point of a small cash boost if you're then trapped in a day-to-day life that you don't love? Money is a tool to get you a life you enjoy and nothing more.

You can prepare yourself, so that you're ready to take advantage if luck strikes for you in a way that works for your personal situation. If you manage to buy a home and that place goes up in value, there are ways to take advantage of the increase in value beyond just selling up.

Money is a tool to get you a life you enjoy and nothing more.

If your house is technically worth more, the bank might be more willing to lend you money to start up your own business. That is the difference between paper and real wealth, right there. If you start a business that does well, you're getting money through the door, rather than relying on capital gains.

IF YOU HAVE BEEN paying off your home, and you've built up 30 to 40 per cent equity, then maybe you only realise that when you sell. Ultimately, you want to use that equity to your advantage. You can leverage that to buy another investment property or start a business.

You take the value embedded in your property and use it as collateral to start a business. You use that to your advantage, and we define that as leverage. Now obviously there are risks around that, you're using your home as collateral. Let's say you start a business and it falls over, you may have to sell your house to cover the costs – so leverage is not without risk. But it does give you the ability to take those sorts of risks.

If you want to use leverage, make sure you leave yourself an equity buffer; don't tap into the full value of your house. In some ways, that's diversifying as well. Then even if the housing market goes backwards you have your business. That's diversifying risk.

I always go on about the need for productive assets, and a business and employing people, that's very productive for the economy as well, instead of potentially just buying houses that sit there.

Mark Fowler – Hobson Wealth Partners

Equity How much you own of something (often used to refer to house ownership).

SOME PEOPLE DO THE same thing to get an investment property. Just bear in mind that you're playing with debt, which can be a risky situation. But these are options you should know about.

While we're at it, this idea of paper wealth doesn't just apply to houses. Shares go up in value all the time, but I don't want to sell mine – not yet, not for decades. Like I've said, my strategy is to buy and hold, so an increase in my shares' value is more paper wealth.

I don't want to kill the goose by selling my shares. I want those golden egg dividends.

14.

A rising tide lifts all boats

NOW THAT WE'VE ADDRESSED budgeting, money mindset and investing, we're finally ready to talk about pay. It's still true that if you don't sort your head out, no raise in the world will help you. But *of course* life is easier when you also get more money coming through the front door.

Before we start the pay talk, I want to be clear – life isn't fair and there is all sorts of discrimination you can face in life. I myself have walked smack into the glass ceiling on occasion.

This is one of the reasons people sometimes get angry about personal finance advice. When you're talking about it in public, you're always talking about the general rules of the game. In New Zealand, this is a legal requirement – you need to make sure people understand anything you say is general money advice, and for anything personal to them, they should talk to an expert about their own situation. But that disclaimer is easily lost in the noise of daily life.

Money is such a personal topic that people get rightly annoyed when they see articles that seem to ignore that the playing field isn't level for all of us.

While you can make the commitment to argue for a pay rise, to cut back on spending and to put the difference into smart investments, some of us will have a harder time with this than others. It's not fair. Life sometimes isn't.

There are all sorts of fun ways you can be discriminated against. Your age is one. Data from Stats NZ in 2017 shows you earn the most between the ages of 40 and 44. But when the people in their late forties and early fifties are nowhere near retirement, you have to wonder what's happening to them. If you talk to people in their sixties, you'll also hear plenty of anecdotes from people who can't get a job, no matter how many they apply for.

In order for that data to be fair, everyone in their late forties onwards would be voluntarily cutting back on hours or switching to a lower position. I just don't believe that. It's a red flag for ageism.

There's also classism. I still remember the sharp sting of outrage when, towards the tail end of 2017, I read that Fonterra's then CEO Theo Spierings had almost doubled his pay packet to $8 million a year.

I've never had a 100 per cent pay rise before. I certainly haven't had one worth $4 million.

Theo Spierings was not a one-off situation either. University of Otago research has found that between 1997 and 2015, chief executives' pay packets increased 228 per cent. Over the same time period, they found the average worker's pay went up 91 per cent.

Sure, you need good leadership, but you also need people to do the actual work. It seems extremely unfair that the people already paid the most are getting increasingly bigger slices of the pie.

Then there's the gender pay gap. Oh, but people love to deny this exists. Never mind that there's cold, hard proof. In 2018, Stats NZ found that women are paid 9.2 per cent less than men, on average. The gap is worse for Māori and Pacific women. If you're in a job considered 'highly paid', the gap widens again, to women being paid 20 per cent less.

Just like the problems with ageism and classism, the gender pay gap isn't just because of the 'choices' women make either. A major study was released in March 2017, commissioned by the government and carried out by the New Zealand Work Research Institute, AUT and the University of Waikato.

The things that people usually blame, like the differences in education, women picking lower-paid jobs or going to part-time work to raise a family, only accounted for 20 per cent of the pay gap in New Zealand.

That huge 80 per cent left to explain? The researchers said it was caused by differences in behaviour between men and women, as well as either conscious or unconscious bias against women. To put that in plain talk, it was because of sexism.

Meanwhile, research published in the *Harvard Business Review* in June 2018 found that women ask for a raise just as often as men do. They're just turned down more often, so there goes another myth.

As a side note, if you run a business; treating people fairly increases how invested your employees feel and therefore how hard they work for you. In a number of different studies, employing a diverse range of different people has been proven to increase profits. If you're worried about the pay gap at your business, Strategic Pay has a free tool to help you identify if you've accidentally got a problem. Why not at least check it out? (www.strategicpay.co.nz)

Anyway, none of these fun ways you can be discriminated against are a reason to give up. Nope, they're reasons to arm yourself with every weapon in your arsenal, including joining a union and pushing for wider social change, if you're that way inclined. You've also got options if you want to go it alone.

The first place I like to start is arming myself with knowledge. It's helpful to have an idea of average pay rates when you ask for a raise. You never know, you could discover you're being unrealistic, or you could find evidence that you're being underpaid. Hard figures are always helpful.

While lots of other countries have places where you can find salary data, New Zealand is a bit trickier. There's no central, open platform with information about average pay rates for everyone. There are workarounds though. You can talk to other people around you to see if they're willing to tell you how much they're being paid. It's one of the best strategies to know not only pay rates, but pay rates within your company. Just be careful about it; some bosses won't like that – for obvious reasons.

Knowledge is power. Find out pay rates through your union, industry associations or just by talking to others working in the same field.

You can also get in touch with the union for your industry and ask them. They collect information about pay rates and are a bit more reliable than friends who might play their own rates up or down, depending on how they feel about money.

It's important to do your research, then sit down and plan out what you want to say, before asking for a meeting with your boss.

SAY YOU WANT A 10 per cent pay increase. You need to work out what other people are getting, what the justification for the raise is and some kind of statistics that you can depend on. That kind of research is quite important.

You can also tell your personal story – how long you've worked for the company, what you do to add value, how long it's been since your last increase and why you need it. It depends on the employer, but some of those personal stories are quite powerful.

If there's something that's more important to you than money, talk to them about that – maybe training, childcare, even transport to work in some industries. If your employer really can't do anything with the money because of their financial position, then talk to them about what you would have been doing with that money. Maybe it's easier for them to help you with something like that.

I would also point out that, internationally, the pay gap between unionised and non-unionised workers is 20 per cent.

John Ryall – assistant national secretary, E tū Union

OF COURSE, THERE'S THE possibility that the place where you work doesn't want to work with you on pay rates. It doesn't hurt to research your other options, just in case things go south. Sometimes the only good thing for your career is to go elsewhere. But you have other options before it gets to that.

'In the bargaining that I've done over the years,' John says, 'and I've done a lot of it, I've always stood by the motto "speak softly, but carry a big stick." You don't have to do something dramatic, but you should think strategically all the way through it. Do your research, look at the points of leverage you have and use those points.

'Remember that you're going in there every day, and you hope to keep working with them for the next umpteen years after this, so do work on those relationships as you go. We'll say to employers, we're not trying to kill you, and hopefully you're not trying to kill us. We just want something reasonable, and we are actually here to negotiate.'

Yes, it's a horrible feeling to ask for that meeting, and then go in there and justify how much you're worth to the company. No, it's not exactly an equal power relationship. I don't know about you, but I'm not a person who enjoys difficult conversations, particularly when they're about money, and particularly when they're with people you'll have to keep seeing day in and day out.

But that's no excuse for avoiding them.

Don't forget, inflation means that the same amount of money is gradually worth less over time. If you don't bring it up and push for more, you'll likely end up going backwards. It's not fair, but as my mum used to say, 'life's not fair'.

If you don't want to talk to the union, there are other options. Strategic Pay CEO John McGill says many professional associations do surveys of pay rates, as do recruitment companies and job sites like Seek and Trade Me. They won't cover every career, much less every job within that career, but they can be another helpful place to look for information. Just bear in mind that when you get free information, it can be of varying quality.

John says it's worth remembering you're well within your rights to raise pay with the boss, as long as you're prepared and positive about it. You also need to pick your timing; asking for a quiet word around the time of pay reviews or performance management reviews is often the best idea.

AT THE END OF the day, your view on what you're worth is just your view, and that's a brutal reality. We all have the ability to negotiate, although the employer usually does have greater resources than the individual, so you need to be able to give the employer some information and make the case for what your issues are.

From the employer's perspective they've got affordability issues to think about, or the pay system may well have a pay scale or grade. Knowing how that system works, not just for you, and how those decisions are made won't do any harm. That's where the employer is coming from.

You're always dealing with imperfect information, but so is your boss. They don't know everything about you and what you're thinking, but what they should know is what your performance is like and what colleagues doing similar work are getting. You should have an understanding of what you're doing in this job, how that is measured, and what the employer is looking for. You can ask what other people are getting, but politely.

They have a pot of money and they do want to allocate that as fairly and as reasonably as possible, but what's fair might be a matter of opinion, based on different factors.

John McGill – chief executive officer, Strategic Pay

I GOT ADVICE WHEN I was younger that the best thing you could do in a negotiation was to look at things from the other person's point of view. Then you argue in ways that make sense to them.

Maybe you want a raise because you've got a kid on the way or you want to buy a house. Those are great reasons – to you. Your boss doesn't really care, not from a business point of view. Again, that's life. Work with the world you're in, not the one you'd like to be in.

Have you brought more money into the business? Improved a system, made something work better or quicker? Do you have a spotless safety record? Think about what matters to your boss, then argue that point. It's much more persuasive, and it's the only thing I've personally found to work.

I am absolutely shameless about this and keep a 'show-off' file for my work. It has the dates and names of big wins I got for the company and the results it brought in the door. That way I can brush up before a meeting, ensuring I don't forget anything.

It also means that if you check your show-off file and find it's looking a little lean, you get a reminder to pick up your game. Hey, everyone coasts now and then – but you can't coast right before asking for a raise.

A good one can also be asking your boss what sort of performance they would like to see to make sure you're earning that extra money. It makes it clear that you're happy to bring value for them, but that you expect to be rewarded for it. After all, you're not at work for the fun of it. You're not a volunteer at a charity. You're there to earn a living, and you have every right to expect fair pay for that.

John McGill agrees that keeping the show-off file is a good idea. Because while a good employer should be watching the work you do, things could be missed. The person who's paying the most attention to your career is you.

IF YOU HAVE THAT information to hand, that's a very good reminder. Make sure you've got that note and be prepared to use it. The other person across the table might only remember you coming to their attention when you messed up a couple of things. They should be reminded of the good things too. Put your case, as well as possible, and explain yourself concisely. If some things haven't gone as well as they could have, make sure you're prepared to talk about why that happened as well.

Just don't go into that conversation without preparation. You've got to be prepared to manage your own career, otherwise you're doing yourself a huge disservice.

Even if you don't have huge expectations about what you want to do, you've still got to be positive and proactive in being good at your job. I've employed a lot of people over the years, and attitude is everything, no matter what level.

There is also a stage that is a bit more risky, and that's to get into some serious negotiating. I've done it in my career and sometimes had it done to me by my employees. You may be thinking of leaving, you may have had a job offer. If you have a reason to want to stay where you are, then lay that on the table.

I'd suggest that you be very well prepared and have a plan B if it doesn't work. From time to time, it's the right opportunity to take. You have to be prepared when those moments come up, to look after yourself and state your case. Done well, it works, you just have to know what you are doing and have thought it through. Sometimes you'll have to be prepared to leave the organisation. Sometimes it is the right decision.

John McGill – Strategic Pay

THIS COMES UP TIME and again – you need all the information you can get, and then you have to take your courage in your hands and back yourself. So many of the tricks and tips I've found have come from honest conversations with co-workers. Often, I've only found the courage to advocate for myself after having an honest conversation with someone, and then finding out I should be getting paid more.

Also, it's one thing to ask for a raise in your current job, but if you're looking at a new job, don't you dare take the first figure offered without at least talking about it.

Changing jobs is the best time to talk salary and your best chance at getting a higher one. Don't bring it up in the first interview or anything that makes you look grabby. But once you're agreed on whether you're the right fit for the job or not, it's time to negotiate money. You are valuable and you're allowed to stick up for yourself. You're proving to your employer that you know how to do your research and stick up for what you're worth. Those are good skills that you'll also use on their behalf at work. Don't be shy to show them off.

Their goal is to save money – your goal is to make money. Don't ever take the first offer, because they'll have offered you less, expecting you to negotiate. Try not to say how much you currently earn and don't name the figure that you want for working for them. The person who says a number first loses.

And for the love of god, be pleasant all the way through this, even if you sometimes have to vent to a friend between the negotiations. A spoonful of sugar helps the medicine, etcetera etcetera. Pleasant, polite, but prepared and firm.

None of this is reason to be mad – you just need to know how it works. Otherwise, you could definitely end up in a situation where you're feeling mad.

My husband faced exactly this dilemma when he changed jobs. He had worked for the police, but hit a dead end and was ready to do something different. I've spent my career in the private sector, where you quickly learn that if you don't ask, you sure as hell don't get. He was leaving a job where pay was never negotiated, it was just set. He was moving into a private sector role with pay bands, but negotiation within those bands.

We'd talked about the job and I'd briefed him on the general idea of negotiation. You don't bring up pay unless they do and it's usually once you've been offered the job. You don't accept the first number offered to you. You let them name the first number, then you counter with a higher one.

This was all well and good, except he froze from inexperience. When they called to offer him the job, the HR woman breezily told him he was the preferred candidate, here was how much money they were offering and asked what email should she send the paperwork through to. She then thanked him and hung up.

When he hung up the phone, I was a little confused. Did she mention money? What happened? Why didn't you say anything?

A little unkind, as he then became flustered and thought he'd blown the negotiation. Of course, he hadn't. He steeled himself for the conversation then sent an email saying he'd like to discuss pay. They called him back.

He explained that he would like the top of the pay band because of the experience he was bringing to the role. The HR woman didn't skip a beat, told him she'd need to clear it with those in charge of the budget, and called him back within an hour to tell him that it had been approved.

Look, I can't promise it will always be that easy, but I can promise that bosses expect you to negotiate your pay. If you don't do it, you're missing out on thousands – maybe tens of thousands.

Even if you are already in your current job and you didn't negotiate at the beginning, it's never too late. A close friend of mine suspected that her husband was being underpaid in his job. She tried to encourage him to ask for a raise. He resisted it for months.

Eventually, he brought it up with the boss. His boss was at first confused and asked how much my friend's husband was being paid – only to be quite shocked when he was told the number, immediately agreeing to a raise.

Your boss is busy. They're not going through individual files, checking everyone is being paid the right amount for the job they're doing. They're usually focused on fighting the daily fires that come up in business. The person who's paying the most attention to your situation is you. Advocate for yourself or you'll get lost in the million other things that your boss needs to do.

Conversations with other people have helped me endlessly, so now I try to pay it forwards. I'm quite open about my salary these days, at least with people I know and trust. I'm not sharing any information with the guy who puts fish pie in the work microwave, but I'll have honest chats with just about anyone else.

I'm naturally quite a secretive person, particularly with money, but then I think many of us are. It can be difficult to get used to, and, yes, it can be awkward when there's a big difference in pay levels. But when you know what those around you are getting paid, it's easier to guess your value and argue your case to the boss.

Advocate for yourself or you'll get lost in the million other things that your boss needs to do.

I've had people tell me you shouldn't do this, and not one of them has convinced me. It can create a toxic work environment, some say, when you compare and someone comes out on top.

True, but it's not the employees who need to justify why they're getting paid differently for doing the same work. When other people have turned out to be getting paid more than me, it's not them I'm mad at, it's the person who decided we were worth such different amounts. Why wouldn't my co-worker argue for the most they could get and then take it?

It's on the boss to justify why someone might be getting a lot more. If they have a reason, such as my colleague has more experience or a niche skill, then fine. If the employer can't justify the difference? Well, gosh, maybe it's time for me to pony up.

As John McGill mentioned, there's always the option of pushing the big red nuclear button and quitting your job. It's a fair option, and I've used it once in a crunch, but it's one that you should treat with caution. Have you been in this job for long enough that it won't raise red flags with new employers? Are you going to quit in a way that means you still get a good reference in the future?

Most importantly, do you truly have another job to go to? Do you have enough money to tide you over while you look for a new one? If you threaten to quit unless you're paid more, your boss might accept. If you're bluffing, then you're in trouble. Competition for you is great leverage and one of the only times that you as the employee has more power. But don't bluff.

All of this talk about pay isn't some academic debate, or a case of earning more so that you can blow it on cocktails at happy hour. Pay snowballs over time, so you have to make sure you stay on top of it. If you miss a couple of important pay bumps, you might be okay now. But what happens when you reach a new, expensive life stage, like kids or buying a house? You can't suddenly jump three pay levels.

You also need to be paid what you're worth throughout your lifetime, so that you can be prepared for the future – to save, invest and, eventually, retire. Research into the gender pay gap shows exactly why this matters. Because most women are paid less throughout their working lives, many more of them face the grim reality of spending their old age in poverty.

In 2017, ANZ released a report looking at the first 10 years of KiwiSaver. It stated that 'if a woman had done nothing differently but be born a man', she would have $79,000 more in her KiwiSaver by retirement. For average pay rates at that time, it means a woman would have to spend three years saving literally every cent she had (after tax) to make up the difference. When you look at the percentages, the average woman's

KiwiSaver account balance is 19 per cent lower.

Keep in mind that currently ANZ is New Zealand's largest KiwiSaver provider – they have a lot of data to look at.

We've talked already about how beautiful compound interest is. Compounding returns on investments mean that if you start earlier, the money you make gets added back into the pot of investments, so the bigger pot earns you more for next time, which also gets added back into the pot of investments . . . it's a delightful snowball that mostly just needs time.

But compounding can also make debt and inequality worse. When you're being paid less, the pay gap also gets compounded. What starts as a small difference between you and your co-workers can stretch into a gulf the size of the Grand Canyon by the time you retire.

You may or may not be a woman, but this shows why it's important to be paid what you're worth. Small differences soon become big ones. You can't control everything. But you can make sure that for the things you can control, you keep a hold of them.

Discrimination takes many forms, but the gender pay gap is the easiest to demonstrate with because there are good, reliable figures on it. If you suspect you're being underpaid, for whatever reason, now is the time to do what you can. There are also wider social changes that need to happen, no doubt about it, but there's no reason why you can't do both at the same time.

Maybe you can't totally bridge the pay gap all by yourself, but maybe you can make it better than it would have been otherwise.

Getting extra (job-focused) qualifications, working hard to

get a raise, going into negotiations or the job hunt for a raise are all really important. I'm keeping my fingers crossed for you. But don't forget that when you get that extra income, you need to sit down and work out a budget, so that you're living below your means. Otherwise all of that extra work for the extra money was a waste.

15.

Get used to plain talk

KNOWLEDGE IS POWER – it's a saying for a reason. What you'll be seeing by now is the things that seem small and simple quickly get you ahead in life as long as you have the discipline to regularly put them into practice.

As I started making changes in my life, I saw that each little gain worked together with other little gains and together they were powerful. The trick is turning these things into habits.

Creating a habit becomes easier when you get mindset right, and mindset is easier when you take away the taboos around money. We need to talk about it, guys. We're not only missing out on the tricks people around us are using, but anything that we don't talk about is something we feel weird about.

I still find it hard to listen to early 'Cooking the Books'

podcasts because part of the show's concept was for me to talk about my own experiences on air. You can hear the discomfort creeping into my voice the first few times I did this. But truly, it only took a few episodes before it started to become easier and easier. Within a few weeks, I started talking about money more in real life as well. I didn't take the stigma away before feeling okay to talk about it. It took talking about it before the stigma in my mind went away. I just had to start doing it and eventually my brain caught up.

I suspect part of the silence around money is because it is tied up with so many things that cut to the core of us. How valuable we think we are. How important we think we are. How smart we think we are. But when I started talking frankly to other people around me about my own mistakes, it gave them permission to do the same.

Now, I was not only learning from the experts interviewed on my show. I was learning bits and pieces from the people around me, and that was just as valuable. How can you ask a question if you don't know a certain subject exists? People would bring things up with me in conversation that I'd never thought about, then I could go away and research it on my own time.

In her podcast, 'Bad With Money', Gaby Dunn infamously had her first episode start with asking strangers on the street their favourite sex positions. All of them answered, giggling nervously, but happy to share.

Then she asked them how much was in their bank accounts – and every one of them clammed up.

Money taps into the most fragile part of us – our self-worth. Everybody seems to shut up out of fear of looking stupid. It leads to a certain viciousness when people do speak up about their mistakes. You can see the comments for news stories online, flooded with accusations the person is a moron, that they brought their problems on themselves. As if being nasty to other people will save us from making the same mistakes, show the world that we know better.

And heck, so what if they did bring it on themselves? I also brought it on myself when I climbed a tree I shouldn't have then fell out of it. People do dumb things, otherwise life would be no fun. You still take each other to the hospital to get fixed up.

I truly believe the secretiveness about money is hurting us more than it's helping us. Yes, you get to avoid some embarrassment, but I was the most secretive when I was being the most reckless. Deciding to talk openly about money came at the same time as deciding I needed to do better and hold myself to a higher standard.

In fact, for years into our relationship, my husband and I had separate finances. As I write this, we've been together 15 years, yet we only fully combined our finances in the last year.

I was the one who was in favour of the separate accounts (Ben didn't really care either way) and I always put it down to a determination to be in control of my own situation. Nobody tells me what to do, least of all with my money, but the way we've combined our finances now I've still maintained my financial independence. There are plenty of ways to do that.

Only as I've addressed my own financial behaviours head on have I realised that one of the reasons for keeping totally separate bank accounts was to ensure privacy – or more accurately, secrecy. When I impulse bought, he had no idea how much or on what. I was just suddenly, mysteriously broke – and looking cute in a new dress.

As I've trained myself to stop overspending, to resist destructive impulse buying, I've become more open. I still slip up with impulse buying from time to time because that's life, but I'm not hiding it anymore and we just deal with it together. We didn't have to combine finances to do that, but when I stopped trying to hide everything, combining suddenly made more sense for our situation. What I've also realised is how this has taken a pressure off our relationship. He doesn't feel shut out anymore, lied to. People know when you're hiding things, even if they don't confront you about it.

It turns out I was guilty of very low level financial infidelity, and it's lucky I got my act together because it's a nasty relationship killer.

Financial infidelity means lying to your partner about money, possibly hiding spending, hiding debt you owe, opening secret bank accounts, maybe even taking joint finances to spend on things that you haven't cleared with your partner. Financial infidelity can also turn into financial abuse, where finances are used to control the other person. It's sneaky, it's shady, and it can not only ruin your relationship, but also your partner's credit score and future prospects.

It's a long swimming pool and I was certainly at the shallow end of it. I didn't run up any debts or steal money, but the secrecy and personal overspending could easily have created trust issues.

A 2016 American study conducted by Harris Poll on behalf of the National Endowment for Financial Education found that 42 per cent of adults had committed some kind of financial infidelity. Of those, 75 per cent of them said it had hurt their relationship. That study found that while the high-end deceptions caused big problems, the smaller ones were still bad. Arguments and loss of trust were just the beginning, with some relationships ending in divorce because of it.

If you're on the other side of the financial infidelity issue, there are some red flags that might confirm your suspicions. Finding receipts for purchases you don't remember, not seeing bills, or your partner getting defensive or refusing to talk about money are among them.

You need to be on the same team, so try to bring it up in a way that they don't feel ambushed. Remember, money for many people is a symbol of worth, which ties deeply into personal identity and power dynamics in the relationship. Have a think about how you can get back on the same page. It's important – for both of you.

It's not a disagreement about what you want to do with your money. That's perfectly reasonable. I have a high risk tolerance and make my own individual investments without ever running them past my husband. But my monthly investment budget is an agreed amount that comes out of the joint account and into my personal investing account. Then I do what I like with it.

I no longer twist my phone away from Ben while checking my bank balance. If I messed up my budget by impulsively buying something I shouldn't have, I'd sigh and say, 'Look, I really wanted it, but I can't go out to the movies for the rest of the month. You go for it, if you want.'

Changing this felt like a weight had been lifted off my

shoulders. I was no longer battling a rising tide on my own.

I'm far more open with the other people in my life as well. I still have issues with spending impulsively or wanting to do fun things with my friends when I don't necessarily have the cash for it. But it was freeing to stop fudging excuses, or worse, going into overdraft to try to keep up. To say, 'Actually, I'm short this week, so I can't go out for breakfast, but let's have a coffee and go for a walk.'

It turned out that literally nobody cared. They just switched plans with me. I'd been tying myself into pretzels for absolutely no reason. I'd been worried about embarrassment, when nobody but me really cared about my money situation.

AUT finance lecturer Dr Ayesha Scott says people often think of the money taboo as existing between households, but many people won't even talk about money with their closest family members. 'We don't have these conversations with our children. We didn't have them with our parents, so to expect two individuals to come together in a relationship, having never openly talked about their financial situation, that's a big ask.

But you're going into a relationship where, in the eyes of the law, everything is shared – debt, income, assets, KiwiSaver. This is why money issues can be a real source of relationship disharmony. It's a leading cause of divorce.'

It's not just *a leading* cause of divorce; many studies have found it's the *number one* cause of divorce. Part of it is the stress simply driving people apart. Part of it is people seeing each other as the problem, rather than the money, and blaming each other for their problems. Instead, they could team up and attack the money problems together. There are a minority of people in these studies who found money problems brought them closer together because they worked as a team to fix them. If you're talking and working together, that can be you. Life's stresses don't have to drive you apart.

By not talking about it, we bury our heads in the sand. It allows us to avoid even being honest with ourselves.

Of course, when you've never talked about money before, there is some adjustment as you peel the Band-Aid off. My husband and I moved in together when we were practically still kids, just before my eighteenth birthday. When it came to talking about the grocery shopping or the rent, neither of us knew what we were doing. For a few years there, any time money was brought up, it would inevitably become a fight because we both immediately tensed up.

I'm confident assuming that's a pattern that will feel familiar to many people. It wasn't a conversation we were comfortable with, and so any comments were ripe for being taken in the worst possible way. Recipe for disaster, right there – even between two people who love each other.

I'm a 'grab the bull by the horns' kind of girl, so once I realised money was a touchy subject in our house, I simply started bringing up money all the time. I wanted to desensitise both of us so that money became a normal thing to talk about. Big things, small things, I just kept working money into the conversation. It did work, although I would point out my relationship has survived my being fairly blunt and impatient on many fronts.

Luckily, there's research on how to become more open about money while keeping these teething issues to a minimum.

WE ATTACH A REALLY high amount of emotion to money, how much people contribute and how we spend it. So to have those positive conversations you almost need to start these things on the sly, start small. You need to start a positive track record to break that pattern of blame and emotion that creeps in almost immediately with money.

People will say, 'Oh, you should have money dates' where you regularly talk about your finances with your significant other. This is true, but what's missing is how do you have that conversation in a real relationship where sometimes communication is difficult? Money can be fraught. The average couple doesn't talk about money enough, let alone in a way that is constructive.

You don't have to start with restructuring the mortgage. Talking about what you imagine life will be like when you retire can be a good one because we all have some vision of what that might look like. If you start with where you want to end up then it becomes easier to look at where you are now and whether you're on track to meet that goal.

Other people like to start talking about it with, 'What would you do if you won Lotto?' Because that can be really telling for whether you're on the same page about your goals in life. You can start these conversations to turn money into something that unites you. It shouldn't be something that divides you.

Dr Ayesha Scott – AUT

ONCE YOU'RE INTO THAT conversation, or when you start having the harder ones, there are still ways and ways of talking about this. Once again, those clever researchers have already tried and tested a few different techniques. Sarah Sanders published research in 'Wire' in 2015, which showed some good ones that work for most people. Remember that you're a team, so rather than saying '*you* need to . . .' maybe try, 'If *we* want to go on that holiday, I think *we* need to cut xyz from our budget.'

Forget about point scoring or 'winning' the debate. Try to avoid exaggerations like saying your partner *always* does something. You'll get much further if you start with the goal you both want to hit and work backwards to find ways to achieve it that work for both of you. You might even have different ways that you're individually working towards the goal, but you should each know what the other is up to, so that you're not undoing each other's hard work.

You may think this is nothing to do with you, that you are able to talk money to your significant other and nobody else need know your business, that people who want to learn more about money should simply read the financial pages or books like this.

This book is full of my own personal journey and that's for a reason. When you talk openly about your own relationship with money, and what different people have achieved with different tactics, it's much more powerful than simply debating finance theories back and forth.

Smartshares CEO Hugh Stevens is involved with investor education as part of his job. He says the most powerful learning tool is people hearing personal stories.

'You can talk about dry financial topics all day long, put graphics around it, be as articulate as you want, but a technical, rational discussion is never going to win. The thing that works in financial education is real people, telling real stories.

'The problem there can be that people are very willing to tell their positive stories, but not their negative ones. For example, I've just been going around the country for an investment seminar series. This one man came up to me afterward with his wife, and they had saucer-shaped eyes.

'He said, "Oh, we wish we came to this a week earlier because we just sold our house, and we're not settling on our new house for two months. So we took all of the money from our settlement and put it into shares." This was at the beginning of October [2018], when there'd been a market correction, so they'd lost 10 per cent of the value of their house.

'The problem then was he immediately crystallised his loss. As soon as the shares went down, he pulled out and put the money into cash. So when the market bounced back the very next day he didn't get the benefit.'

If you were to listen to the tape of this interview, you would have difficulty making out what Hugh is saying because all you can hear is me talking over the top of him: 'Oh no. No. *NO*. Oh, they didn't. No.'

That story is almost step by step what you should not do. We've already talked about it, so you'll know: shares are a long-term investment, if the market goes down you hold tight, and don't yank your money out in a panic. This poor person broke every one of those rules and I'm sure they regret it deeply.

That's exactly why it's so important to share these stories. How else can you save other people from repeating your mistakes? Why should you suffer in shame and silence? Mistakes happen – help others avoid them. Maybe you'll avoid a few clunkers when other people around you share theirs.

PEOPLE NEED TO HEAR those types of stories, and know what can happen if you don't follow some rules. Because they might hear that you invest for the long term, so then you can ride out market ups and downs. If you're investing for the short term, then cash and fixed interest are better options because your money is protected. But it's one thing to hear that and another to do it because people tend to look at the past returns of a share fund and think, 'Wow! Imagine if I got 20 per cent . . . ' They forget the rest when they don't have someone's experience to remind them.

Hugh Stevens – Smartshares

ANOTHER REASON IT'S IMPORTANT for us to start talking is illuminated by a piece of research by BNZ in 2017, which found a third of New Zealanders had no money plan. People just had this airy fairy idea that they would be fine. But even for the 68 per cent of New Zealanders who said they had a financial plan, only 34 per cent knew how much we needed for retirement.

Well then, I'm sorry, the rest of you don't have a plan.

You have to sit down and write this stuff out. You can't just think to yourself, 'Oh, yes, I've got this . . . ' without checking whether you actually *have* got this. Funnily enough, talking to other people can also be the way to snap you out of this.

Always write out any money plans. They can look very different on paper.

Living between Auckland and Hamilton for work is great for my lifestyle, but it also means I need two places to lay my head at night. At first, I airily informed my husband that I planned to leverage off our home to buy a leasehold apartment.

Leasehold properties can be a good investment in some circumstances, as they are cheaper. You're not buying the land underneath the property, you lease it (hence the name). That means any rental returns become a higher percentage return because you put in a lower amount to start with. It also means you pay an ongoing cost for the land, as well as paying back your mortgage. For this reason, it almost always is a bad idea to buy leasehold, but there are a minority of cases where it can work.

Ben repeatedly expressed his doubts, but I assured him I'd thought through the numbers and it would be fine. We could put the apartment on Airbnb when I wasn't there.

It was only when we sat down, talked honestly and wrote down the numbers involved that I realised I was very, very wrong. There was no way we could afford that. The numbers did not add up.

I ended up renting a room off a friend, for cheap, because I'm there less than half the time. She gets a flatmate who's a ghost, and I get two houses that feel like a home and have people living there who I like spending time with. Thank goodness Ben and I had an honest talk and wrote things down because that could have gone very badly.

Back to that BNZ research because I'm afraid it gets worse. They found that an increasing number of people didn't have enough money to cover an unexpected bill. Those under 30, like I was when the research was released, were the worst offenders.

Only 17 per cent of people in my age group had a concrete future plan for their money. This is worrying. We've already talked about how the magic of compound returns means you make the most serious cash, with the least effort, when you're young. But those who are younger probably have no idea they're throwing valuable time away – nobody warns you about that. I only found out when I started researching it myself.

Don't start ragging on the young ones too soon though. The research found that even the oldies weren't doing well. Of those between 50 and 64 years old, 59 per cent said they didn't know how much they would need for retirement. They were right on the doorstep of it, yet avoiding looking at a problem that was too hard and too scary.

When nobody around you is talking about it, it can be easy to convince yourself that nobody else is worrying and it seems to be working out just fine. But I'll bet good money that those doing the best are putting their money to work behind the scenes.

By not mentioning your money issues to anyone else, you miss the knowledge that could be all around you. You also avoid having to admit it to yourself that anything is going wrong. The people around us can often help, even just by pointing you in the right direction to find answers. By not talking, you're cutting yourself off from doing better.

When I was avoiding talking about money, it was a nagging stress always at the back of my mind. I knew it wasn't good. Finally taking back the control was an empowering rush, especially when I found out just how simple some of the changes could be.

We also need to talk to each other because there's no one else who will do this for us. Research from the Commission for Financial Capability shows several worrying trends. It shows that 73 per cent of people leaving high school have either learned nothing or very little about money. It also shows that 82 per cent of school leavers wish they'd been taught more and feel out of their depth. There's a real consequence to that mismatch – 16 to 24 year olds are the most vulnerable to taking on unmanageable amounts of debt. The compound interest on that debt can quickly spiral. Some don't financially recover. Ever.

I hope that scares you. It scares me. It also breaks my heart for them.

Amanda Morrall once worked as a personal finance journalist in New Zealand, before writing a personal finance book – *Money Matters: Get Your Life & $$$ Sorted* – and going on to work at the KiwiSaver provider Simplicity. She says the biggest problem in personal finance is usually procrastination. Sometimes it's driven by fear and people not knowing where to start. When people haven't talked about money their entire life, they don't know what the first step is. Even looking for information can be daunting.

'The thing that I see all the time, particularly with younger women, is this fearfulness. Then that turns into procrastination. But with personal finance, you procrastinate at your own peril.'

Amanda is a mother, and is tackling this problem ahead of time by making sure she openly talks to her kids about money.

ON A DAILY BASIS, there's always an opportunity to talk about money. There's a dialogue in the household, and many kids don't have that dialogue full stop – forget about KiwiSaver, just money alone. Education does start from a very young age.

You start by making it part of the household conversation, basically. There are always tiny little lessons. I bring my kids grocery shopping with me, and I send them off to get things. Initially, they would just grab whatever, so now I'm training them to look at the price and make comparisons. It's an easy thing that they can understand.

Then you take it to another level when they're able to, and when it comes up, you talk to them about rent or mortgages, bill payments. Then as milestones come up, like buying a car, I sit down and make them run the numbers themselves, so that they can understand that.

It's very easy for a parent – if you have wealth – to just pay for things, but you're not doing your kids any favours, unless you want to be paying for your kids when they're in their forties. Or you can be really miserly, and make your kids earn everything and pay for everything on their own. It's more finding a balance where you have those conversations, and money isn't taboo. Money shouldn't be a fearful topic, but one that the kids are excited and interested in.

Amanda Morrall – author of *Money Matters*

AMANDA'S RIGHT. HOW ELSE will they learn? If you don't talk to your kids about money, some idiot might be doing it instead.

Obviously there are limitations to this. If a random person calls you up and asks for your bank details, don't tell them.

Same for your scammy uncle who likes to ask for a loan, ‘because I know you can afford it’.

You don’t need to talk to people about how much you’re paid, unless you’re comfortable to do so. You should also be balancing the things you hear on the grapevine with some reading of your own, from the many experts writing books and articles. And don’t be that person who learns about personal finance and starts lecturing everyone around them. Nobody likes that guy.

Learning to talk about money when it comes up means we’re all sharing the tips we’ve learned along the way. At the risk of being cheesy, we all have to do our part in making the world a little bit better, and sharing our experiences with other people is part of that. The more selfish part is that if you share your experiences with other people, they often share theirs right back. The more people you talk to, the bigger picture you start to get of what’s working in the real world.

Get over the money talk discomfort; it doesn’t last long.

16.

Find your people

AS I TALK ABOUT the changes I made in my life, it might sound like I think this is easy stuff. Just learn the error of your ways! See the light and make the switch! Stop being so wasteful with your money – gosh, I'd never thought of that before, I think I'll give it a try!

Of course it's hard. Life gets in the way. Willpower runs low. You run out of mental energy to keep all the balls in the air.

Even as I write this, I'm not totally free of my bad money instincts. I still automatically want to impulse buy things, particularly on a bad day, and then hide the financial damage. But I am at the stage where I can consciously overrule that impulse, knowing it only buys misery. I'm hopeful that one day the mindset change will become a habit.

Until then, that extra mental effort is so worth it. My story shows that any idiot can get it together and learn more about money. This idiot did.

I've had people ask me where my sudden personal finance knowledge came from. If I took a paper or an online course. People who I catch up with after a few years express surprise that I'm suddenly so interested in money and seem to have answers to their questions about it.

The answer is a combination of a few factors. I'm still not an expert, but I had access to experts, and have had many fascinating conversations with them where I was lucky enough to be able to ask them whatever I wanted to.

As it turns out, the basics of personal finance aren't all that complicated. Truly. You can drill down to layers where it can get tricky, if that floats your boat – but you don't need to. In terms of learning enough to know how to improve your situation, to know where you want to go? I truly believe anyone can do it. You don't need to take a course or become qualified as a financial adviser to know how your finances work. The harder part is just doing it and doing it consistently.

I didn't change my relationship with money so that I could be rich and live a fancy life. I'm also not interested in giving up all material things; some of them are very enjoyable. It's somewhere between the two, where you take control to get the life you want. No more, no less. By taking control, I make sure I have the resources to keep my life the way I want it, long term, whatever life throws at me.

There are always things out of our control, and not everybody can turn themselves into a millionaire overnight, but almost all of us can at least improve our situation. For the things we can't change by ourselves, learning more about money means that we can at least push for the bigger social changes needed for more people to get ahead.

I've been lucky plenty of times in life and I'm honest about that. There's no denying it, really. But changing the way I use money, and improving my knowledge about it, means that I'm alert and ready to make the most of it when new opportunities turn up. If the opportunities I've had so far hadn't materialised, then I couldn't have got here on my own. But I'd still be in a better position than I'd started in. Such is life.

Many of us need a helping hand from time to time. Make sure you pass it along by helping up other people you see who need it.

The times when it's just willpower and life getting in the way are the times when you need your community. The people who help you remember that no, your success in life isn't measured by the size of your house, that you can reward yourself with something other than first class flights to Bali, that the simple joys in life often cost nothing and taste the sweetest.

The internet has brought us many horrors, but it's also helped many of us to find our people. I've cultivated friendships where we can talk honestly about what's happening with our money and I've joined a few online communities. The Mustachian and Early Retirement communities have a strong presence online, and just joining a few Facebook groups has meant I get a regular dose of motivation when I'm mindlessly scrolling.

Many of these people are chasing the dream of FIRE: Financial Independence, Retire Early. The idea is that you reduce your living costs, invest your new savings and eventually your investments will be earning you enough money that you don't need to work at all. Some of them are planning to quit their jobs at 30 or 40 years old.

Then there are those who only want the financial independence part; getting to the point where they have enough money to pick and choose the work they find most fulfilling and do it on their own terms. That's probably the category I'd put myself in. I love my job, but I don't ever want to be trapped in it.

The idea isn't necessarily a rejection of work. It's an embrace of life. It's a movement of people putting in the foundations so that they can live a life on their terms, where they work hard when they need to, but not slavishly, and they don't miss out on the rest of life that all of that work should make possible.

You can get more of almost anything in life, except time. You exchange your time working, for money. If you decide to stop spending as much time working to pay for things you don't want, then you can have more time for the things that actually matter. If you make your money start working harder as well, then you get even more time back. It's about priorities.

This isn't some crazy idea that only exists in other countries, where the rules or life situations are different. Alpha Leung is a New Zealander who I first met through one of these Facebook groups. He manages family life on a budget while living in expensive old Auckland and documents the journey on his blog, The Smart and Lazy.

He says retirement doesn't have to be about age, but your financial situation.

I FIRST STARTED THINKING about it after we had a baby, and my wife stopped working for a while. I saw my money going backwards. I took a closer look and realised, 'Oh, I'm spending all my money without even noticing'.

The simplicity of the FIRE movement is boiled down to a single factor: your saving rate. Saving rate is the percentage of your income – after your expenses – that you put away. You're paying attention to your spending, and then always making the most of your savings.

If you spend 100 per cent of your income then you can never be retired, because you'll always need that income. But if you manage to save money and invest it wisely, the money will keep growing by itself until it hits a point where you can basically live off your investment forever.

Alpha Leung – The Smart and Lazy

IT'S NOT THAT ALPHA doesn't have bills to pay and a life to live. As well as a mortgage, he has two kids, but he doesn't believe he has to choose between looking after his family and living a frugal, investment-savvy life.

'It's a choice, how you spend your money. You just need to pay attention to where you spend it and things change a lot. That spending, it felt like nothing. Getting rid of it, we didn't feel any different.

'Some people think the nice stuff will give you happiness, but what I think is the freedom and how I spend time with my family is what gives me happiness.'

Both Alpha and I have been inspired by the online FIRE

community and the generosity of people sharing the money tips that work for them. Alpha puts that generous spirit down to people realising that the early retirement dream is achievable, and that they don't need to compete with each other.

'They realise they don't need to wait 20 to 30 years to retire or be a multi-millionaire to retire. You can achieve financial freedom if you're willing to make some small but important changes in your life.

'When you work, you trade your time for money. But you stop using your money to buy stuff, and use to it buy your freedom and time. We buy our life back, so we don't have to live according to our jobs and that income.

'On the other hand, it's not a get rich quick scheme. The principal of FIRE is to increase your income, minimise your expenses, and invest wisely. It's good old-fashioned money tips, and that's why it resonates with people.

'Do you want to trade most of your adult life for work, so you can have a nice big house, and a nice big car? Or invest your money wisely so you can reclaim your time, and do whatever brings you happiness?'

Alpha is planning to hit his early retirement when his kids are in their teens, letting him enjoy family life fully while they are still around. Frankly, it doesn't get better than that.

Alpha's story isn't a tall tale from one person who hit it lucky or hid help that he got from elsewhere. Nick Carr is a financial freedom coach and registered financial adviser. He also blogs about his own journey to FIRE at Your Money Blueprint (yourmoneyblueprint.co.nz).

He wants to achieve financial freedom by 50, which is

ambitious considering he didn't discover the early retirement community until he was in his mid-thirties. He has a family and lives on a fairly average income, but says it's never too late to start.

'Early retirement, to me, means having enough money to live the life I want to live without worrying about where my next dollar is going to come from. I prefer to call it financial independence. I don't actually want to retire early, that's too all-or-nothing. But I'm seriously considering if I might want a career change in my mid-forties. There are levels to this, where some people have enough money to confidently take risks or pursue their passions to get what they want out of life. If you can get that sooner rather than later, why wouldn't you?

'Money is just the vehicle to get you to your destination. I want to do things that make me the happiest. Things like spending time with my daughter, to play tennis in the middle of the day if I want to, just that freedom. Money's not the end goal, it's what the money can buy, which is time for me.

'Some people look for the jobs where they earn the most no matter what the job is, because they're spending so much, and need the money to live. But once you lower your expenses, money becomes less important. It's the freedom money gets you, the freedom and options and time.'

Nick started slowly, first cutting down his budget just a bit. But he's now ramped up to save 50 per cent of his income each week, thanks to a focus on his biggest expenses.

'Your savings rate is just the gap between what you earn and what you spend, and the bigger the gap, the sooner you'll hit retirement. If you earn $80,000, and save $40,000, then your savings rate is 50 per cent.

'There's a common rule in the [early retirement] community that you need to save 25 times your annual expenses. The theory is that that money will be enough, if invested in enough growth assets that it will last you for the rest of your life. For most people, if you manage to save 50 per cent, that will get you to 25 times expenses in about 17 years. That's a fine starting point, but I'm aiming for 30 times, just to be on the safe side.

'So that's the number, but as for the strategy, you have two levers. You can increase your income or you can decrease your expenses. Cutting back on spending is the lowest hanging fruit. You're not always in control of your income, but you can track your spending. For a lot of people, that's eye-opening.

'I used geography to lower my cost of living. For those familiar with Wellington, I used to live in Churton Park. I had bought too much house, as much as I could afford, but it was too much for me. I moved to Wainuiomata, which is a much lower cost of living area, the house was about a third of the price. I went from 190 square metres to 90 – just a small three-bedroom place.

'Because it was a smaller house, the rates were lower, then insurance was lower, smaller electricity bills. I managed to score a job with a work vehicle, so that's another large expense gone. From one simple move, I managed to cut $30,000 from my annual expenses.

'A house is a house to me, it's just a place to live, it doesn't affect my happiness. Whereas if I went full throttle in cutting out nice food or other things that bring me happiness, that would be more of a sacrifice to me. It was easier for me to save

$15,000 a year on the house, than save $2000 a year scrimping on food.'

Nick still tracks his spending to make sure he's spending only on the things that bring him happiness and not wasting money on things he doesn't care about. He negotiated new deals for other core expenses including power and internet.

It hasn't just been cutting back though. Nick has also put his best foot forward at work, getting three promotions in five years, and started his side business as a financial freedom coach. The coaching is a passion that he would eventually like to do full time, even though it would mean a pay cut. For now, it's the extra income that helps to get him closer. He's the first to admit that he needed both to increase the income *and* reduce the expenses.

'It's not just enough to, sure, save 30 per cent of your income. That's great, but if you don't put that money somewhere productive it's going to end up as nothing. Investing in the stock market has been a great growth mechanism for me. I'm a big fan of index investing, which means a wide range of funds across the world, diversified, low fee. That's been the home for basically 90 per cent of my money while it's growing.'

All of these changes came about after a fairly unfortunate hallelujah moment. Nick herniated a disc in his back and was off work for six months. ACC covered many of his expenses, but not all of them. As he started to panic about money, he realised he was dependent on spending every cent of the wages coming in the door each week.

'I was 33 and it hit me that I was too old to be having those money problems. Sometimes you have to have that moment of desperation to change your mindset, which is a bit of a shame. I had a mortgage and I was worried about the house being taken off me. In a sense, I'm glad that happened. Otherwise I'd still be not thinking about this stuff. It was that panic which helped me out in the end.

'You don't have to go from zero to 50 percent savings right away. It's a gradual thing. Just get started, really. It can be difficult to get started when you see people ahead of the game, but don't compare yourself to others. Just get started, and hopefully you'll end up as someone that others are looking up to.'

People in early retirement communities, like Alpha and Nick, are inspirations. They help each other calculate the cheapest life insurance, share power tips, the best cheap groceries going at the moment. Whenever I'm running low on willpower or discipline, one of the posts will inevitably pop up in my Facebook feed, discussing the finer points of cell phone plans or what investment is giving the best return at the moment.

When I need an expert, I'll flick on a personal finance podcast on my walk to work, or browse the business section of the newspaper. The two combined give a powerful dose of motivation and information. You need those regular hits when you're trying to make a change.

It's important that I've found a community that motivates me, because I'm still me, and I'm still someone who's prone to making snap decisions. This can include buying things I shouldn't, 'forgetting' to put money into savings or thinking that one month off won't hurt. Inevitably, it's not just one month off. It can derail me entirely.

These guys are better with numbers than I am, they're willing to go without more of life's luxuries than I am, and are willing to share how they got there. The kindness of these communities means it very rarely feels judgemental. In a digital world with ads shouting at you to buy more every five seconds, an online safe haven is a welcome panacea. Just because the rules of money management are simple, doesn't mean it's easy to actually do. These people keep me on the straight and narrow.

I admit, I'm not what most people would consider a FIRE devotee. I love my job and don't want to quit any time soon, but imagine reaching the stage of financial independence where your job is some sort of quirky hobby. That's what I want.

Surrounding myself with people who are more dedicated than me keeps me going when I want to stop. It shifts my definition of what's normal, so my middle ground isn't just 'don't get into debt', but 'do some good stuff with your money, too'.

Now it's your turn. You've got this.

Glossary

An incomplete list of the weird and wonderful words of finance

ACTIVE VERSUS PASSIVE INVESTING

Active investing means you buy and sell regularly, continuously monitoring the area you invest in, to try to get ahead of the game. Passive investing is the opposite. Investors try to pick a good long-term investment then leave it alone to do its thing, avoiding the fees of buying and selling, and also avoiding rash emotional decisions. Research shows passive investing earns more profits over time.

BONDS

One of the lower risk type of investments, where your money is unlikely to go down, but you also only make a smaller return. Usually they are government bonds, and, technically, the money you invest is a loan to them. They then pay you back at a fixed rate with interest. You'll sometimes hear them referred to as a 'fixed income investment' because you know how much you're getting and when. Of course, the price for that certainty is a smaller return on your money.

BUY AND HOLD

A strategy of passive investing, but that more accurately describes what the investor is doing. You buy investments and hold them for a longer period of time, no matter what the market is doing in the short term.

CAPITAL GAIN

The increase in what something is worth, which you only earn when you sell that thing. If you sell a house for more than you paid for it, that is capital gain. Rental income is not capital gain. Selling a share for more than you paid for it is capital gain. A dividend is not capital gain. It is also possible to make a capital loss if you sell when the market has gone down. Capital gain is the opposite of investment income.

COMPOUNDING RETURNS

A beautiful way to make money by using time to your advantage. Any investment earnings or profits are reinvested, and therefore also earn more money. You're earning money not only on what you invested, but also on the money you've accumulated from those investments. You can use compounding to your advantage with term deposits, shares, houses, any type of investment. The most important thing is giving it as much time as possible for the snowball to get bigger.

CONSERVATIVE VERSUS GROWTH INVESTMENT

Conservative investing aims to reduce the possibility of losing the initial investment by investing in less risky assets. The price is a lower return or earnings on that investment. Good for those who may need their money back within the next year or two. Growth investing aims to maximise profits by investing in riskier assets that might go up and down in the short term, but earn more over the long term. The price is a bit of a rollercoaster ride. Good for those who have five or 10 years, maybe longer, until they need the invested money back.

CORRECTION

A word experts use for when the market goes down. 'The market is going through a correction' sounds less scary than 'Arrrgghhh! Where has all my money gone?' The idea is that what is going through a 'correction' must have been overvalued in the first place and is now 'correcting' back to its actual worth.

DIVERSIFICATION

Buying more than one thing, or not putting all your eggs in one basket. The idea is that if you buy more than one type of investment, you protect yourself from bad luck with one of them. Bad investments are a fact of life, as are car crashes if you drive. Diversification is the equivalent of getting insurance.

DIVIDEND

A cash payout to people who own a share in a company. It normally comes from that company's profits. Not all companies pay a dividend, and the amount that is paid can vary wildly. In New Zealand, dividends are usually paid out twice a year. Information on what dividend returns you can expect can usually be found when you buy the share in the first place.

EQUITIES

Equities, shares, stocks, all the same. It's referring to the fact that when you buy a share, you own a little piece of that business. Hence you have a bit of equity in it, so you have invested in equities.

EQUITY

How much you own of something. Often used to refer to a house; if you have paid off 20 per cent of it, and the bank is still loaning you 80 per cent, then you have 20 per cent equity.

FMA

The Financial Markets Authority. They're New Zealand's money sheriffs, in charge of taking down the bad guys and keeping us safe from the scammers.

INDEX FUND

An automated type of investment fund, which automatically tracks and invests in a certain area. An example is the NZX50 index, which invests in the top 50 companies in New Zealand at any one time. The aim is to give a broader market exposure, diversification, for a low cost.

INVESTMENT INCOME

Money that you make while you hold an investment asset. Rent from an investment property is investment income. Making lots when you sell the house is not. A share dividend is investment income. Selling that share for a profit is not. This is the opposite investment earning strategy from capital gain.

LEVERAGING

Using debt to make an investment. Often used in conversation to mean using the value of your house to borrow more money from the bank, to then invest in something like an investment property or starting a business. Because it uses debt, this is a more advanced technique than many think. If you use leverage to start a business and the business fails, you could lose your home. Only use with care.

LIQUIDITY/ILLIQUIDITY

How easily you can turn something into cash. On the scale, property is closer to illiquid – you have to sell the entire thing or nothing at all, and you have to wait until you find a willing buyer. A savings account is highly liquid – you can walk into your bank and ask for the money back at almost any time.

MANAGED OR MUTUAL FUND

An investment fund run by a person, so usually charges more than an index fund because a real person is involved and making the decision. People gotta get paid! Your money is pooled with money from other investors and then spread across a few different investments that the fund manager thinks will do well.

RETURN

How much your investment makes for you, the profit, how much money 'returns' to your pocket. You can get a return from earnings as you go or from capital gain. For a house, you could make money from the rent or you might only make money when you sell and it's hopefully gone up in value. Certain shares are more likely to give you a high dividend or more likely to go up in value for when you sell them.

RETURN ON INVESTMENT

Similar to the above, but applied to your specific investments. The aim is to work out what percentage you are getting back, compared to how much you invested in the first place. You take how much you have overall, subtract how much you put in. That number is the profit you've made. Then you divide your profit number by how much you put in in the first place. Multiply that by 100 and the result should be a percentage. It sounds more complicated than it is. You use it to figure out how successfully different investments are performing.

RISK

Risk is anything that puts you at risk of losing your money. However, I'd argue that your definition of risk should be personalised to you. If you panic during volatility, that's a risk. Leaving your money in a low-interest bank account, so that its value is eaten away over time, is a risk. Figure out what is risky for *you*.

SHARES

Shares are a unit of ownership in a particular company or financial asset. You buy a piece of that company, your share of it. 'Buying equities' means almost the exact same and is referring to buying shares.

TERM DEPOSIT

Money you give to the bank to hold for a certain length of time. At the time of writing, interest rates are low, so term deposits are a secure but low-return investment. If interest rates go up, they may become a better investment depending on what's happening in the rest of the finance world.

VOLATILITY

How much an investment will go up and down. Just like someone with a volatile temper can be calm one minute and shouting the next, a volatile investment can be making bank one moment and down in the dumps the next. Volatility is *not* the same as risk or return, but the three can be closely linked. High risk investments are often more volatile, but can make you a bigger return. But not always.

Bibliography

Financial knowledge

‘ANZ research shows nearly a quarter of New Zealanders have no savings’, ANZ news release, 20 April 2018, www.anz.co.nz

‘Are today’s young people super savers or splurging spenders?’ Treasury staff insight, 19 July 2016, https://treasury.govt.nz/publications/research-and-commentary/rangitaki-blog/are-todays-young-people-super-savers-or-splurging-spenders

‘She’ll be right, but will you? BNZ calls for New Zealanders to remember their financial basics’, BNZ media release, 27 April 2017, www.bnz.co.nz

Frances Cook, ‘Why a simple savings account is the key to money happiness’, *New Zealand Herald*, 25 April 2018

Financial knowledge and behaviour survey, Commission for Financial Literacy, 2013, www.cffc.org.nz/assets/Documents/FKBS-2013-June-Financial-Knowledge-and-Behaviour-Survey-Summary.pdf

Alex Neill, et al. (2015), ‘The financial capability of secondary students, and the place of financial capability in secondary schools’, New Zealand Council for Educational Research

Financial behaviour

‘22nd annual quantitative analysis of investor behaviour 2015’, Dalbar, www.qidllc.com/wp-content/uploads/2016/02/2016-Dalbar-QAIB-Report.pdf

‘Issues and concerns for Australian relationships today’, Relationships indicators survey 2011, Relationships Australia

Brad Barber & Terrance Odean (1998), ‘Boys will be boys: gender, overconfidence, and common stock investment’, https://ssrn.com/abstract=139415

Credit Karma, 16 November 2017, www.creditkarma.com/studies/i/stress-spending-study

Tim Devaney, 'Survey: more than half of US respondents caught in cycle of stress spending'

Edwin Elton, et al. (2017), 'Target date funds: what's under the hood?', Center for Retirement Research at Boston College, 17:2

Johannes Haushofer & Ernst Fehr (2014), 'On the psychology of poverty', *Science*, 344:6186, DOI: 10.1126/science.1232491

Andrew Jebb, et al. (2018), 'Happiness, income satiation and turning points around the world', *Nature Human Behaviour*, 2

Daniel Kahneman & Amos Tversky (1979), 'Prospect theory: an analysis of decision under risk', *Econometrica*, 47:2, DOI: 10.2307/1914185

Tim Kasser & Aaron Ahuvia (2002), 'Materialistic values and wellbeing in business students', *European Journal of Social Psychology*, 32, DOI: 10.1002/ejsp.85

Brad Klontz, et al. (2011), 'Money beliefs and financial behaviors: development of the Klontz money script inventory', *Journal of Financial Therapy*, 2:1, DOI: 10.4148/jft.v2i1.451

Mark Riepe, 'Does market timing work?' Charles Schwab, 16 December 2013, www.schwab.com/resource-center/insights/content/does-market-timing-work

Celeste Robb-Nicholson, 'Writing about emotions may ease stress and trauma', Harvard Health Publishing, n.d., www.health.harvard.edu/healthbeat/writing-about-emotions-may-ease-stress-and-trauma

Sarah Sanders, 'Strong beginnings, financial equals', Wire women's information project report, June 2015, www.wire.org.au/strong-beginnings-financial-equals

William Sharpe (1975), 'Likely gains from market timing', *Financial Analysts Journal*, 31:2, www.jstor.org/stable/4477805

Jennifer Sheehy-Skeffington & Jessica Rae, 'How poverty affects people's decision-making process,' Joseph Rowntree Foundation, 1 February 2017, www.jrf.org.uk/report/how-poverty-affects-peoples-decision-making-processes

M Tatzel (2002), '"Money worlds" and well-being: An integration of money dispositions, materialism and price-related behaviour', *Journal of Economic Psychology*, 23:1, DOI:10.1016/S0167-4870(01)00069-1

Research on household spending

'2015 characteristics of new housing', US Department of Housing, www.census.gov/construction/chars/pdf/c25ann2015.pdf

'Consumer expenditures 2017', Bureau of Labor Statistics, 11 September 2011

'Household expenditure statistics: year ended June 2016', Stats NZ, 2 December 2016

'New Zealand retirement expenditure guidelines', Massey University Fin-Ed Centre, June 2017, www.massey.ac.nz

'NZ ranks worst in global survey of car value depreciation, MTA blames two-tiered market', *New Zealand Herald*, 8 February 2017

'Self-storage services: Australia market research report', IbisWorld, August 2018, www.ibisworld.com.au/industry-trends/specialised-market-research-reports/consumer-goods-services/self-storage-services.html

'We're building bigger 40 years on', Stats NZ, http://archive.stats.govt.nz/browse_for_stats/industry_sectors/Construction/building-bigger-5oct-16.aspx

Marc Bain, 'Why is make up so expensive?', *Quartz*, 2 November 2015, https://qz.com/537730/why-is-makeup-so-expensive/

Tamsyn Parker, 'Kiwis worry about record level of debt', *New Zealand Herald*, 19 August 2017

Data that impacts your finances

'Gender pay gap is second smallest', Stats NZ, 15 August 2018, www.stats.govt.nz/news/gender-pay-gap-is-second-smallest

'Research of the gender pay gap in New Zealand', The Ministry for Women, https://women.govt.nz/work-skills/income/gender-pay-gap/research-evidence-gap-new-zealand

Benjamin Arts, et al., 'Research: women ask for raises as often as men, but are less likely to get them', *Harvard Business Review*, 25 June 2018

Ben Leahy, 'Affordable homes selling fastest across NZ due to first home buyer interest: QV', *New Zealand Herald*, 1 August 2018

Corazon Miller, '45% rise: property values jump across Auckland region', *New Zealand Herald*, 16 November 2017

Gail Pacheco, et al. (2017), 'Empirical evidence of the gender pay gap in New Zealand', The Ministry for Women

Helen Roberts, 'New Zealand pay ratios', Otago School of Business, www.otago.ac.nz/business/research/department/otago119826.html

Aimee Shaw, 'Wage by age: how much should you expect to earn at your current age?', *New Zealand Herald*, 7 April 2017

Finance companies

'Attitudes towards New Zealand's financial markets', Investor confidence research, Financial Markets Authority, May 2018

'Dollars and sense – a decade of KiwiSaver', ANZ Investments, September 2017, www.anz.co.nz

'Monthly statistics', Kiwisaver, www.kiwisaver.govt.nz/statistics/monthly/schemes/

Dennis K Berman & Jamie Heller, 'Wall Street's "do nothing" investing revolution', *Wall Street Journal*, 17 October 2016

Eugene Fama & Kenneth French (2010), 'Luck versus skill in the cross-section of mutual fund returns', *The Journal of Finance*, LXV:5

Bart Frijns & Alireza Tourani-Rad (2014), 'The long-run performance of the New Zealand stock markets: 1899–2012', Auckland Centre for Financial Research www.nzfc.ac.nz/archives/2014/papers/programme/II-2b.pdf

—— (2014), 'Kiwisaver: who is really reaping the benefits?' Current Issues in Fund Management, 3:2, doi.org/10.24135/afl.v312.45

Vladyslav Sushko & Grant Turner (2018), 'The implications of passive investing for securities markets', *BIS Quarterly Review*, www.bis.org/publ/qtrpdf/r_qt1803j.htm

Acknowledgements

THE BIGGEST THANK YOU goes to my husband for putting up with being married to a workaholic, who does things like spend her 'summer holiday' writing a book, and who somehow put up with me when I was a money mess. Ben, you have the patience of a saint. Except for the times when you don't.

Thank you to all of the podcast listeners who walk this road with me. For sending me your questions and trusting me to find the answers. Most especially to those who messaged me to tell me you'd tried a new money tip and it worked. I love how much we help each other.

To my mum for being the world's biggest cheerleader, no matter how ill-advised some of my schemes are.

To everyone I've interviewed for this book and the podcast. Thank you for being so generous with the knowledge you've worked hard to build up. My favourite thing about the personal finance community is how the majority of us just want to help other people figure this out. Everyone within these pages proves that.

To Team Pod – heck, it's really just the three of us, making the impossible possible each week. You're life savers. Every girl should be so lucky to have a pair of Chris's to help her out.

To anyone who read this far and is ready to start their own money journey. Change is hard, and you rock for embracing it. Let me know how you go.

Frances Cook
July 2019

Notes

RANDOM HOUSE

UK | USA | Canada | Ireland | Australia
India | New Zealand | South Africa | China

Random House is an imprint of the Penguin Random House group of companies, whose addresses can be found at global.penguinrandomhouse.com.

First published by Penguin Random House New Zealand, 2019

1 3 5 7 9 10 8 6 4 2

Cover design by Kalee Jackson © Penguin Random House New Zealand
Text design by Cat Taylor © Penguin Random House New Zealand
Prepress by Image Centre Group

Printed and bound in Australia by Griffin Press, an Accredited ISO AS/NZS 14001 Environmental Management Systems Printer

A catalogue record for this book is available from the National Library of New Zealand.

ISBN 978-0-14-377380-1
eISBN 978-0-14-377381-8

penguin.co.nz